hope
your
heart
needs

hope your heart needs

52 ENCOURAGING REMINDERS OF HOW GOD CARES FOR YOU

HOLLEY GERTH

Revell

a division of Baker Publishing Group
Grand Rapids, Michigan

© 2018 by Holley Gerth

Published by Revell
a division of Baker Publishing Group
P.O. Box 6287, Grand Rapids, MI 49516-6287
www.revellbooks.com

Printed in the United States of America

Library of Congress Cataloging-in-Publication Data
Names: Gerth, Holley, author.
Title: Hope your heart needs : 52 encouraging reminders of how God cares for
   you / Holley Gerth.
Description: Grand Rapids : Revell-Baker Publishing Group, 2018. | Includes
   bibliographical references and index.
Identifiers: LCCN 2018010009 | ISBN 9780800729547 (cloth : alk. paper)
Subjects: LCSH: Jesus Christ—Name—Biblical teaching—Meditations. | Jesus
   Christ—Name—Anecdotes.
Classification: LCC BT590.N2 G47 2018 | DDC 242/.2—dc23
LC record available at https://lccn.loc.gov/2018010009

Unless otherwise indicated, Scripture quotations are from the Holy Bible, New International Version®. NIV®. Copyright © 1973, 1978, 1984, 2011 by Biblica, Inc.™ Used by permission of Zondervan. All rights reserved worldwide. www.zondervan.com

Scripture quotations labeled KJV are from the King James Version of the Bible.

Scripture quotations labeled NKJV are from the New King James Version®. Copyright © 1982 by Thomas Nelson, Inc. Used by permission. All rights reserved.

Scripture quotations labeled NLT are from the *Holy Bible*, New Living Translation, copyright © 1996, 2004, 2015 by Tyndale House Foundation. Used by permission of Tyndale House Publishers, Inc., Carol Stream, Illinois 60188. All rights reserved.

18   19   20   21   22   23   24   8   7   6   5   4   3   2

Contents

CONTENTS

CONTENTS

Introduction

God is the strength of my heart.

Psalm 73:26

"How are you?"

"I'm fine."

It's the answer we all give. Often what we really mean is, "I'm a little tired. A bit overwhelmed. Longing for something more." In this world, our hearts grow weary. We want hope, joy, peace, and purpose. Surely all of this is around the next corner, we tell ourselves. If we hurry, if we try hard enough, then we'll find it.

One morning I curled up under a cream-colored blanket that felt like the edge of a cloud. I turned on the lamp by my bed and sipped tea from a red cup with a little chip in the rim. I didn't want this day to be like so many before. I wanted to know the answer to the restlessness in my heart. I needed a real solution.

I did an internet search. I texted a friend. But on this occasion, neither of those would do. I reached for my Bible then and flipped through the pages. I began to notice verses about who God is and how he loves us. And suddenly I came to a turning point: I realized what my heart needed wasn't a simple answer to a problem. No, I was looking for, longing for, a Person.

We all are.

Someone bigger than us. Stronger. Able to handle everything. Someone who will care for us, fight on our behalf, and extend grace to us always. Someone limitless and loving, beyond our imagination, and right there in the intimate details of our lives—always the same and yet forever doing a new thing in and through us.

"I already know God," we might say. And, yes, that can be so beautifully true. But thinking we know him completely is like believing we have held every grain of sand from all the shores of the world in our hands. No matter how much we love him, however deep our faith goes, there is always so much more. This is a wonder and a gift. With every new discovery, our hearts are filled and freed, strengthened and helped, restored and empowered.

Or maybe God is still brand new to us. We feel a bit shy around him, like someone on a first date. We want to know more, but our knees are knocking and our heart is pounding. Maybe we've been hurt by religion or don't feel good enough or have a thousand reasons why we want to stop reading and walk away. If so, that's absolutely okay. This is a come-as-you-are book, because that's the kind of God we'll get to know on these pages.

The God who scattered stars like diamonds across the velvet of the universe, the keeper of every sparrow, the maker of us all is inviting us to draw closer to him. He is the place where our hearts can go on the hard days and the happy ones, in the highs and lows, when we are sad or frustrated or downright giddy. He is what we have been searching for all along.

No amount of words could ever even begin to contain all of who God is. What's on these pages is only a sliver. But understanding more of God's character and how he loves us changed my life in beautiful, powerful ways. As you begin this journey, I'm praying it will do the same for you.

We don't have to settle for "I'm fine." Someone is whispering to us, inviting us, showing us in every moment, "I am God. I love you. You are mine."

XOXO
Holley

ONE

Beginning and End

"I am the Alpha and the Omega," says the Lord God, "who is, and who was, and who is to come, the Almighty."

Revelation 1:8

Today, 353,000 babies will be born.[1] All those new lives coming into the world with a cry and a bundle of potential. Eyes blinking into the light, feet kicking, hands grasping. Hair the color of wheat and coal and chocolate and flame.

God will be there for all those beginnings, like an artist watching an unveiling of the canvas. He knit them together in their mother's womb (Ps. 139:13). He was there for your birth too. Close your eyes for a moment and think of it. The God of the universe watched over your coming; he welcomed you into this world.

Today, 151,600 people will die.[2] They will step from this world into what's beyond. There will be tears and mourning. Goodbyes that are a gentle letting go after a long life and others that feel like an early wrenching. And God will be there for all those endings too. Not a single sparrow falls apart from his knowing (Matt. 10:29). How much more true is that of us?

The 7.4 billion of us who are not arriving or departing on this day will go about our business all over this world. We'll turn off alarm clocks or quiet the rooster. We'll pour the coffee or tea. We'll go off to work in an office or a field. Maybe we'll change a newborn's diapers or change the channel on the television in the new retirement home. We'll worry. And dream. Hope. And doubt. We'll feel happy or sad or tired or all of those. And God will be there for all of that too. Every second of our lives.

He was there before we were created. He spoke the world into being as the light-bringer, star-scatterer, and breather of life into the first man's lungs. He will be here long after we are gone, ashes to ashes and dust to dust. He is the God of the past, present, and future. Ours and all of history's.

This means we are never alone. We never have been. We never will be. There will never be a second when we are out of his sight or his care. In everything we have ever faced, he has been there. And in whatever is coming, he will remain.

God is not just *the* beginning. He is *our* beginning. He is our end. He is our everything in between.

Beginning and End,
you are the Alpha and Omega, the start
and the finish. You are the reason I am here.
You will care for me every day of my life,
then take me home to be with you forever.
Thank you that you will be with me always;
nothing can ever separate us. Amen.

TWO

Author

Jesus the author and finisher of our faith.

Hebrews 12:2 KJV

The coffee shop is crowded this morning. I've come back to my hometown, a bustling suburb on the edge of Houston. The spot where I'm now sipping a latte used to be a cow field. Those of us who knew this place years ago lament these alterations, but it is the way of cities to sprawl.

I don't recognize a single face around me, and if I came a hundred times, that would likely still be true. We are all anonymous and yet shoulder to shoulder. A strange paradox. I imagine for a moment one of these fellow coffee drinkers growing curious enough

16

to ask me, "What do you do?" After years of wrestling and wandering, ducking and being hesitant to say it out loud, I think I would say simply, "I'm an author."

In doing so, I would mysteriously be sharing with Jesus a description he also claims as his own. Hebrews 12:2 says he is "the author . . . of our faith." In our modern world, *author* has limited connotations. It's used almost exclusively for those of us who write professionally and publicly in some way. So I wondered a bit about this word when I saw it applied to Jesus. It felt too small. Too simple. Surely there must be more to it. So I dug deeper and discovered an author is a person who starts or creates something (such as a plan or idea).[1] Ah, yes, this makes sense.

> In the beginning was the Word, and the Word was with God, and the Word was God. He was with God in the beginning. Through him all things were made; without him nothing was made that has been made. (John 1:1–3)

In the Sunday-school versions of creation, only God makes it into the narrative and perhaps onto the flannel board. But Jesus was there starting the story of earth, the story of our faith, the story of us. This is wild and unknowable to me. It tastes like mystery and feels like sacred magic. The Word making cranes with long necks and daffodils the color of butter and jellyfish in the deep. The Word inventing laughter and sex and sneezes. The Word already knowing, somehow, that the plot would include a fall and a cross and a rescuing.

Jesus knew not just the beginning but the ending too because Hebrews 12:2 says he is not only the Author; he is also the Finisher. This resonates with me because it means no matter what happens in our crazy world, he is the only one who can put *The End* on the final page of this world. But even then it will not truly be the end. It will only be the beginning of another, even better story—one that goes on forever with us and with him.

When I think of Jesus as the Author in this way, something inside me gives a sigh of relief. Because it means I don't have to hold the pen of my own life, and I can be certain of the One who does. I know he is good and faithful. I know he is wise and kind. I know he is untamable and victorious always. He is not a careless creator. He will take care of every syllable and sentence, every dash and comma. There is a fierceness with which an author loves their work. It is beyond words to describe, but I have felt it in my bones. It is wild and gorgeous to think this is how the Author feels about me, about us. We are not random scribbles on a page. We are not notes jotted down, then crumpled up and tossed away. "We are God's masterpiece" (Eph. 2:10 NLT).

He is not finished with history yet. He is not finished with our stories either.

Author,

you are the One behind the story of everything, and you live in me. This is such a beautiful mystery. I give you the pen of my life today, and I ask you to make it what you want it to be. Amen.

THREE

Bread of Life

Jesus declared, "I am the bread of life. Whoever comes to me will never go hungry."

John 6:35

I stand on a hot Union Square sidewalk in New York City. The scene in front of me is a human parade. Well-dressed mamas pushing babies in posh strollers. Pink-haired teenagers with trendy sunglasses. Tourists snap-snap-snapping photos and yelling, "Smile!" at one another. I am in a city of 8.4 million people. It's a number that's hard for me to even wrap my mind around. I begin to count, "One, two, three, four . . ." then my tummy interrupts to remind me of more important priorities. It's lunchtime and I need to find a restaurant.

I pull out my phone and go to the app I usually use to find places to eat when I travel. When I do a search, the results stun me—over eleven thousand restaurants are here. I suppose that's how many it would take to feed the hungry crowds that will soon walk out of apartments, office buildings, and subway trains on the same mission I'm on now. How is it even possible to feed them all?

The disciples had the same question when Jesus taught a group of five thousand (plus women and children) in ancient Israel one day. Jesus asked Philip, "Where shall we buy bread for these people to eat?" (John 6:5). Philip must have felt the way I did looking at the endless sea of people in New York City, because he replied, "It would take more than half a year's wages to buy enough bread for each one to have a bite!" (v. 7). Andrew doubtfully offered five loaves and two small fish, the lunch of a little boy who apparently overheard the conversation and wanted to help. With the faith of a child, this boy seemed to know what so many of us grown-ups forget: in the hands of Jesus, even a little is enough.

Jesus broke the bread, gave thanks, and fed the crowd with leftovers to spare. Most of us have heard this story before, but one thing stands out to me anew as I revisit it today. Later in this chapter, Jesus said, "I am the bread of life. Whoever comes to me will never go hungry" (v. 35). It's a statement made separately from the scene where the crowd is fed. But the two stories are still connected, and there is a truth we all need to know when we look at them together. It is this: Jesus is enough for everyone. He is the bread broken and passed out to the hungry.

He doesn't act stingy and say, "Sorry, there's only enough of me for a few people." No, he tells everyone to come. He gives himself over and over again. He is a God not of scarcity but of abundance.

I think of this as I look at the people on the streets of New York again. They are a blur of faces to me, a swirl of strangers passing by. But God has every hair on their heads numbered. He knows every care on their minds. He orchestrated their first breaths and will be there for their last. He knows the cravings and the longings and the emptiness inside every human heart, and he says, "Come and eat your fill."

He is not a God of soul starvation but of salvation. He is not cutting portions; he is passing out extra helpings. He is not giving us meager handouts; he is giving us his very self. And there is more than enough for us all.

Bread of Life,
you are the only One who can truly
satisfy the hunger in our hearts. Thank
you for promising that you will do so.
I want to receive whatever it is you
want to give me today. And, most of
all, I want more of you. Amen.

FOUR

Bright Morning Star

I am the . . . bright Morning Star.

Revelation 22:16

The rough wooden boardwalk is cool beneath my feet as I make my way to the sand. The sky is still the thick, deep blue of night, and gray shadows sway in the salty wind. I sleepily take my husband's hand. I'm not a morning person, but we're on vacation and I'm determined to see the sun climb like a rising warrior above the waves at least once.

As we get closer to the shore, we can see more people who have decided to forsake pillows for flip-flops along with us. They sit on huge pieces of stranded driftwood, stroll along the edge of the water with cameras in hand, or sip from coffee cups with dazed looks on their faces. I notice one woman lifting her eyes to the still-night sky and I am curious. What does she see?

When I follow her example, I am greeted by diamonds thrown out on velvet. One star in particular winks brilliantly back at me. I find out later it's actually the planet Venus, otherwise known as the Morning Star. Here is its mystery and beauty: Venus is known for rising in the darkest part of the night, just before dawn.[1]

Jesus said, "I am the . . . bright Morning Star" (Rev. 22:16). This means, among other things, he is not afraid of the deepest dark. He is not frightened by the secret places in our hearts. The ones that haven't seen daylight for years. The kind with the locks on the doors. The sort we don't say out loud or even fully admit to ourselves. He is not running scared from the tragedies in our lives.

He is not backing away from the brokenness and the bitterness and the shattered dreams. He is not intimidated by the monsters under our beds or inside our minds. He is not avoiding the struggles or the addictions. He is not waving his hands in surrender to the enemies of our souls. He is not saying, "This is too much for me."

He is not afraid to step right into the night. Not afraid to even dwell in the middle of it. Because he is light, and in him there is not darkness at all. This means darkness can surround him and he cannot be defeated or diminished by it. He came as a baby into a midnight world and announced his arrival with a shining star. He conquered death in a dark tomb and rolled the stone away, making a way into the brightness for all of us. In the thickest gloom, *the Morning Star rose.*

"The LORD's mercies . . . are new every morning" (Lam. 3:22–23 NKJV). As I watch the sun slip into the morning sky and fill it with gold and flame, I bear witness that these words are true. Venus, the Morning Star that foreshadowed all this light and blazing glory, seems to be more than just a planet; it suddenly also seems to be a promise. A daily reminder from the heart of our Creator that even the deepest night will lead to dawn. The dark cannot win; the light will never be overcome.

Bright Morning Star,
you truly are the Light who comes
into our darkest places. Today I need
you to shine on this area of my life:

_____.

Thank you for your faithfulness and for the
promise that no night will last forever. Amen.

FIVE

Counselor

He will be called Wonderful Counselor.

Isaiah 9:6

I watch my new counseling client step through the door and look around my office. She surveys the desk, bookshelves, and basket by the couch as if searching for a secret. Perhaps she can find my bag of tricks or a set of keys that will magically unlock all her problems. Surely something in this room can explain why our time together will help. I invite her to find a cozy spot and watch her shift her gaze to me with a quizzical look.

She hasn't found what she thought she might and I smile a bit because soon enough she'll understand why. What she wants to see is invisible. It's floating mysteriously and inexplicably in the air between us in the form of words and expressions and pauses filled with silence. Dr. Henry Cloud, a psychologist and author, describes how one of his professors told his class he was going to reveal the one factor that research had proven truly helps clients. Cloud could hardly contain his anticipation. At last, the formula that could cure everything and everyone. He shares what happened next in his book *The Power of the Other*:

> I sat eagerly, waiting to find out the secret of helping people. Here, at last, I would learn that esoteric kernel of wisdom that I had been seeking all of this time. The professor looked at us and said, "It's the relationship. What actually brings about change in people, and the cure, is the relationship between the psychologist and the client," he explained.[1]

When I read this, I nodded, because I remember hearing the same during graduate school. It's probably the only statistic I can reliably recall from that season in my life. Seventy percent of the success in counseling is simply about the bond between the client and counselor.

We can approach religion the same way my client did that first counseling session. We think there must be something we can see, touch, and feel that will give us what our souls long for so deeply. We read certain books, sing particular songs, practice the recommended spiritual disciplines, and follow the rules. Then we become frustrated because nothing seems to be working. And meanwhile the Wonderful Counselor is saying, "It's not about all of that—it's about the relationship between us." When we connect in meaningful ways with Jesus, we cannot help but be changed.

As a counselor, I was taught my role was to help provide certain things for the clients who stepped through my door. I think these reflect so much of what Jesus offers us too. A safe place.

A listening ear.

An encouraging presence.

Truth spoken in love.

Hope for the future.

Jesus goes far beyond this as well. Because he is not an ordinary human counselor; he is *the* Wonderful Counselor. The word *wonderful* in this verse is actually much more powerful than the way we use it today. In the original language, it means to cause great wonder, to be beyond understanding.

Our Counselor knows much more than we can even comprehend.

He loves us more than we can imagine.

He is always inviting us to simply come and connect with him.

Counselor,

*I'm so glad you are there for me anytime
I need help. Today I'm struggling with*

_____,

*and I want to share it with you.
Please give me your wisdom,
encouragement, and care. Amen.*

SIX

Creator

The LORD is the everlasting God,
the Creator of all the earth.

Isaiah 40:28 NLT

Rows of books greet me, spread out like a rainbow. One with a yellow, smiling dragon. Another with a freckle-nosed dog. A third with a fluffy family of bluebirds, necks stretched to the sky mid-song. It's a wordy wonderland otherwise known as the children's section of my local library, and I'm struck by all the creativity—so many imaginations poured out onto pages.

I feel this all over again when a friend and I go to story time with her little girl. We sit on foam squares that fit together like a confetti puzzle. A small crowd of enthusiastic toddlers cheers and laughs and spins in circles as a volunteer reads about a ladybug too lazy to fly. There are blond pigtails, thick ebony curls, fiery braids, and tousled brown bangs. Each child is unlike any other. Every single one a tale of wonder and hope unfolding right there.

I think we can make the idea of "creation" very big. We talk of galaxies and eons and shifting continents. We talk about the darkness hovering over the waters and the coming of light. We imagine a grand spectacle. And, yes, our Creator God is to be worshipped for all that power and majesty. But the parts of creation that stir up the most praise in me these days tend to be the small ones. The giggle of a child. The delightful cover of a book. The cow standing in the middle of a pond on a hot summer day that nods hello as I drive by on my way home. The firefly that lands on the rim of my glass as I sit on the patio in the early evening. The taste of dark chocolate, bitter on my tongue.

And, yes, all the humans who live on this wild, spinning earth. The babies discovering their big toes for the first time. The toddlers with shaky steps. The teenagers with the smiles they're trying to hide. The brides and the mamas and the napping one-hundred-year-old under the quilt. God made all of this, all of us. He made it for his glory. But he also made it for our enjoyment.

My husband and I read this in Ecclesiastes this morning: "So I recommend having fun, because there is nothing better for people in this world than to eat, drink, and enjoy life. That way they will experience some happiness along with all the hard work God gives them under the sun" (Eccles. 8:15 NLT). These words seem quite scandalous to me. But then I think of slick otters playing in a river and the surprising satisfaction of blowing a bubble with chewing gum and the sound of a baby's first chuckle.

I recently finished a sweet book called *When Mischief Came to Town* about a ten-year-old girl, Inge Maria, who comes to live with her stern and unsmiling grandmother. Inge Maria reminds her grandma and the whole town how to be happy again. Toward the end of the story, the grandmother says, "We are told to be mature and behave, and for some silly reason, we believe this means that we can no longer have fun. We forget how to laugh, how to yell, how to run, and worst of all, how to delight in each other's company. I think we . . . have failed to notice that the same Lord God who gave us the strength to work and the wrinkles to frown also gave us the legs to dance and the voices to sing!"[1]

Yes, let's respect and be in awe of this splendid universe God made. But let's also dare to revel in it like children, like toddlers at story time who cheer and laugh and sometimes spin in circles. "In the beginning God created . . ." (Gen. 1:1). Every small wonder in our lives is evidence he still does and another reason for praise.

Creator,

thank you for all the ways I can see
your character, faithfulness, and love
through the world you designed. Help
me to not only live purposefully but
also simply have fun and enjoy your
good gifts with the faith of a child.

SEVEN

Guide

For this God is our God for ever and ever;
he will be our guide even to the end.

Psalm 48:14

The email comes to my inbox and a thousand questions leap into my mind. It looks like an opportunity, but I've learned from experience that things can be more complex and challenging than they seem on the surface. I feel two emotions at once—anticipation and anxiety. What am I supposed to do?

Life is a series of decisions, and perhaps you've had a similar moment. A job offer presents itself, but you're not sure it's the right fit. You could move to another city, but you also like where you are right now. Someone asks you out on a date or extends an invitation to be part of a group and you're curious but also cautious.

As I silently stare at the email in front of me, I think with a sigh, *I need a guide.* In other words, I need someone to show me what to do and where to go. Is this something God would be willing to do for me? I do a quick search on a Scripture site and find that, yes, God is ready and able to direct us. Here are just a few examples:

> In your unfailing love you will lead the people you have redeemed. In your strength you will guide them to your holy dwelling. (Exod. 15:13)

> He guides me along the right paths for his name's sake. (Ps. 23:3)

> You guide me with your counsel. (Ps. 73:24)

> The LORD will guide you always; he will satisfy your needs in a sun-scorched land. (Isa. 58:11)

Whew. I won't need to make this decision alone. I think then of a moment last year in the Dominican Republic. I'd gone with Compassion International to see the work they were doing to release children from poverty in Jesus's name. Each day we'd venture out into a village to visit the home of a child sponsored through Compassion. On this particular day, doing so meant navigating a winding maze of steep stairs down a hillside. I felt sure I could never reach the destination. But then a local leader waved us on with a smile. "I will show you the way," he said. And even though I still had no idea where I was going, I knew everything would be okay.

That's a gift having a guide offers us. It's not that we suddenly know every step or all the answers. It's that we know somehow, someway, we're going to end up where we need to be. Yes, there may be distractions and detours. We might wander off and get ourselves lost for a bit. But someone is always going to bring us back and make sure we reach the destination. Having a guide changes our role in the whole process. Instead of carrying the burden of figuring everything out, our job becomes to simply follow faithfully.

Unlike my experience in the Dominican Republic, on this side of heaven we can't actually see or physically hear our Guide. But I do believe he still leads us in specific, practical ways.

First, he gives us his Word. "Guide me in your truth and teach me" (Ps. 25:5). When making a decision, Scripture can always be our first filter.

Then we can ask for wisdom from fellow believers. "Plans are established by seeking advice; so if you wage war, obtain guidance" (Prov. 20:18).

We can also pay attention to the Holy Spirit within our hearts. "When he, the Spirit of truth, comes, he will guide you into all the truth" (John 16:13).

Once we have done this, it's often time to just take the next step and trust God will redirect and reroute us along the way if needed. "Many are the plans in a person's heart, but it is the LORD's purpose that prevails" (Prov. 19:21).

I take a deep breath and type a reply to the email. I don't give an official response to the request just yet. I still need to think, pray, and process. So I start by asking questions. There's more to understand, but I already feel greater peace knowing the One who already has all the answers is with me, for me, and holds my future in his hands like a trustworthy guide with a treasure map.

Guide,

thank you for being so wise, loving, and
faithful. You have promised to be with me
every step of the way. I especially need your
guidance in _____.
I love you and trust you to get me where
I need to be today and always. Amen.

EIGHT

Helper

Because you are my helper,
I sing for joy in the shadow of your
wings.

Psalm 63:7 NLT

I grew up a city girl, but once a year I got to visit the livestock and rodeo show, a wonderland of farm animals and funnel cakes. On one such trip, I spotted a plump hen in a corner of a coop, feathers fluffed and a surprisingly ferocious look on her face. At first she appeared to be the only occupant, but as her caretaker gently tapped her on the tail feathers, a ball of fuzz attached to delightfully pink feet appeared. "Peep!" declared the chick as if sounding an evacuation alarm, and soon its siblings followed. I counted them—one, two, three, four. It was like watching the old circus act where clown after clown climbs out of a teeny-tiny car. How did they all fit under their mama? And what were they doing there in the first place?

It turns out hens have used this trick for ages. If a hen senses a threat to her brood, she calls her youngsters to herself and tucks them under her wings. It's a smart strategy to evade circling hawks or nosy farmers. These mothers are telling the world, "If you want to get to my kids, you're going to have to come through me first."

This is the imagery the psalmist David used in Psalm 63:7 to describe the kind of help he received from God: "Because you are my helper, I sing for joy in the shadow of your wings." These words may sound strange coming from a warrior king. We might imagine him talking about help in terms of battlefields, swords, and giant-slaying. But this time a mother bird best conveyed what he wanted to express. When we look closer at the word *helper* in Scripture, this begins to make more sense. Sharon Jaynes says in *How Jesus Broke the Rules to Set You Free*:

> The Hebrew word "helper" . . . is ezer. It is derived from the Hebrew word used of God and the Holy Spirit, "azar." Both mean "helper"—one who comes alongside to aid or assist. King David wrote, "O Lord, be my helper" (Psalm 30:10 NASB). . . . Ezer appears twenty-one times in the Old Testament. Two times it is used of the woman in Genesis 27, sixteen times it is used of God or Yahweh as the helper of his people. The remaining three references appear in the books of the prophets, who use it in reference to military aid.[1]

What this speaks to my heart is that the help of God is both tender and powerful. Strong and gentle. Protective and mama-bear fierce. This comforts me because on my toughest days I want someone to not only defend me but also comfort me. I long for someone to not only beat back the bullies but also tuck me into bed. I want someone who will gather me under their feathers not only because of what's circling overhead but also because it is the closest place to their heart.

This is the kind of mysterious and beautiful help we receive from our God. It is help that is near. Help that knows our name. Help that enables us to sing even in the scary, hard moments because we're secure under mighty, merciful wings.

Helper,

thank you for offering not only your strength but also your very self on my behalf. In a world that can be full of uncertainty, you alone are my security. Today I especially need your help with

_____.

I'm so grateful for your covering of love over me. Amen.

NINE

I Am

God said to Moses, "I AM WHO I AM. This is
what you are to say to the Israelites: 'I AM has
sent me to you.'"

Exodus 3:14

This morning I stood on burning-bush ground.
Only I was not Moses in the wilderness. I was a
girl in an office chair with a computer screen in
front of me. On that screen was the face of someone I loved dearly who had been hurt. I had been
brought in to this video meeting to help sort out
the pieces, to set the bones and offer a sling and
wipe away the salty tears with words. I walked
into the room nervous, unsure of how it would go.

There were things to figure out about the future, and the possibilities for anger and conflict and disappointment lay right there like matches in a box we were all trying not to touch.

But instead of those things, at a particular point I felt a certain Presence, a falling of peace like silent snow settling on our hair and shoulders. Sifting down to our hearts. I know this feeling—this kind of moment when the divine intersects the ordinary and suddenly you are in a holy place because heaven is so near you can feel its soothing breath like a mama's kiss on the curve of your neck.

There's a curious thing about these times and it's this: they only happen in the present. I have never felt this way when I have looked back on the past. I have never gotten this sensation when I've been worrying about the future and imagining how it might hold bombs or poisoned lollipops or squirrels leaping into the road. I have only ever really found God in the *now*.

A lot of very smart scholars have debated about why God calls himself "I AM." Many of them probably know far more than I do when it comes to what can be looked up in books or found on ancient scrolls. But I can tell you with the best kind of knowing I have, which is real-life experience, that I believe part of this name has to do with how God is somehow, mysteriously always present tense. He didn't say to Moses, "Tell them 'I was' sent me to you" or "Tell them 'I will be' sent me to you." No, instead, he insisted, "Tell them 'I AM' sent me to you.'"

Sometimes when I look back with regret at the past or toward tomorrow with fear, it can be disturbing because I can't seem to find God in those places. And I think all the while he might be saying, "I was there when you were. And I will be there when you arrive at that place tomorrow. But right now I'm right here."

Elmer Towns writes in *The Ultimate Guide to the Names of God*, "The significance of this name [I AM] is that Jehovah . . . is and will become to us exactly what we need when we feel that need."[1] This is true all through the New Testament too. When our hearts are hungry, Jesus says, "*I am* the bread of life" (John 6:35, emphasis added). When darkness comes to our lives, he says, "*I am* the light of the world" (John 8:12, emphasis added). When we feel like we've lost our way, he says, "*I am* the good Shepherd" (John 10:11, emphasis added). Whatever you need right now, Jesus is saying, "I am . . ." He's not only present; he's actively providing in this very second.

The meeting eventually wrapped up, and as I stepped out of that little room and into the great big world again, I thought about this beautiful mystery: whatever year, month, or moment it may be, our God is with us. The burning bush is inside us. And wherever we are standing right now is holy ground.

I Am,

it's so comforting to know you are here with me and you promise to provide for my every need. Help me not to focus on the past or fear the future but instead fully embrace this moment. I trust you with all my yesterdays, all my tomorrows, and right now too. Amen.

TEN

Abba

> And because we are his children, God has sent
> the Spirit of his Son into our hearts, prompting
> us to call out, "Abba, Father."
>
> Galatians 4:6 NLT

My husband's cell phone rings and as he answers,
I overhear a single word, *Dad* . . . He tilts his head
with concern as he listens, and I watch him nod in
understanding. I know this is our daughter calling,
which might seem like an ordinary, everyday thing.
But for us, and her, it is not. Because God brought
her into our lives when she was in her twenties
and the word *Dad* is still new in her mouth and
in our ears.

Her story is one of longing—for a home, a family, parents to call her own. We spent years longing for a child before God answered that desire with her. So all of this feels like a miracle to us, like an if-we-blink-it-might-all-go-away kind of wonder. Truly becoming a family has taken time, of course, and lots of healing. And perhaps the way she says *Dad* shows that more than anything else.

At first she did not say this word at all. She barely knew my husband and her walls were high. Then she uttered it with hesitation, as if it had a question mark after it. Perhaps even with a bit of fear and doubt in her voice. But the day finally came when she declared it with a smile and an exclamation point—"Dad!" Now she says it all the time. When she's happy. When she's sad. When she's lonely. When she needs something. I've heard it in every pitch and tone, notes of a song she's finally learned to sing.

On this particular day, she's having trouble with her car. My husband hangs up, grabs his keys, and announces he's going to help. It's a small thing, easily solved. But she tells us later how much it means to be able to call someone, to call a father, and know that he will come.

Her journey reminds me so much of how it is with our hearts. It can take us so long to know how much we're loved, to believe we're really invited into the presence of the One who spoke the stars into place. Yet Paul tells us, "God has sent the Spirit of his Son into our hearts, prompting us to call out, 'Abba, Father'" (Gal. 4:6 NLT). It's beautiful to me that this verse doesn't simply say, "Father." The word *father* indicates a position, but *Abba* reveals so much more.

Easton's Bible Dictionary says *Abba* "is a term expressing warm affection and . . . confidence."[1] The same entry also notes, "It has no perfect equivalent in our language." I nod at this because it's so true. There is no perfect equivalent to the kind of dad that God is to us. Even the best ones will let us down, because they are imperfect humans and so are we. But our hearts can always know we have an Abba who is inviting us to come to him, to call on him when we're in need or afraid or overflowing with joy. Not with hesitation, uncertainty, or fear but with wide-open arms and even exclamation points. Because we really are his beloved children, adopted into his family forever.

Abba,

it's such a gift to know that you look on me with affection and desire to be a true father to me in the ways my heart longs for most. Help me trust your love and believe with every part of me that I really am your beloved, cherished child. Amen.

ELEVEN

Friend

I have called you friends.
John 15:15

She shows up at the coffee shop with a smile on
her face and takes her seat at our little round table,
a circle of friends. "How are you?" someone asks,
and she responds with the usual, "Oh, I'm fine."
But the weariness in her eyes makes the words
ring hollow.

We don't press her, but as she settles in and
starts to feel safe, the smile fades. She begins to
share about the challenges and discouragement,
battles and heart bankruptcy, lies that roar at her

like lions in a cage. She knows they can't really hurt her, but they're unsettling. It's hard to rest.

We lean in and listen hard. We talk about similar seasons in our own lives. I remind them of how just a few months ago I found myself at the doctor and counselor again because depression and anxiety kept taking cheap shots at me. An uppercut to the jaw, a punch to the gut in the moments when I should have felt glad and grateful. "Yes, this world is a jungle and battlefield. And there's no shame in finding yourself in a fight for your own heart," I say.

Then we tell her what is true about who she really is. We remind her that she is strong and brave and loved. We point to her gifts and cue the stories of how she's making a difference. We say these things over and over because when the lions roar, our hearts become overwhelmed and afraid. Then someone makes a funny remark and the tension breaks into the confetti of laughter. She smiles, for real this time, and sniffles into a tissue. Her shoulders drop and I know she's going to be okay. Someone reaches for her hand across the table and we pray fierce words on her behalf.

This is what friends do for each other. They say, "Talk to me. Tell me what's really going on in your world." They listen without judgment or leaving. They look for the best in us, like miners panning for gold. They speak the eternal reality when all that's temporary—emotions, circumstances, opinions—are telling an entirely different story. They sit by us and stay by us and pray for us when we can't do these things for ourselves.

When I consider what friendship really means, I think it comes down to this one thing: true friends are *for* us no matter what. They are not crossing their arms and saying, "I knew she couldn't do it." They are not passing the gossip along with the potato salad at the Sunday picnic. They are not wondering when we'll get over it but instead how they can walk with us through it.

When I think of Jesus being a friend to us in these ways, it changes everything.

It's easy to think of Jesus as powerful, mighty, and holy. It's simpler for me to bend my knee than dare to bend his ear about my daily, ordinary struggles. But we are his friends. We can go to him with anything and everything. We can trust he'll be there to love, encourage, and support us.

We are his friends too. This means I want to be sure I'm not doing all the talking. I want to understand what Jesus is passionate about, what causes him pain, what brings him joy. I want to know all the parts of his heart.

Our little group finishes our lattes and stands up to hug each other before we head for the door. "Thank you," my friend whispers in my ear. "Anytime," I say. "We're friends."

Friend,

*it's still a stunning realization to know
I can call you by that name. Thank you
for wanting to be part of my life in an
intimate, personal way. Please help me to
be a loyal, faithful friend to you too. Amen.*

TWELVE

Shepherd

The LORD is my shepherd, I lack nothing.
    He makes me lie down in green
        pastures,
he leads me beside quiet waters,
    he refreshes my soul.

Psalm 23:1–3

I let the closet door quietly click closed behind me. I sit on the soft carpet in this unseen square of space and draw up my knees to my chest. I let the tears fall, not caring if they make dark rivers of my carefully applied mascara. I'm at a retreat for a group of women and all has not gone well. I'm the speaker for the weekend and have just finished my first session. None of the technology worked right. I felt flustered and distracted. I failed to make coherent small talk during the breaks.

I'd tried so hard to impress this group. I wore my cutest outfits. I curled my hair until I smelled the sizzle of it. I put on three coats of lip gloss and smiled like a small-town beauty queen on a parade float. And because of all this, I can almost guarantee that if I told someone at that retreat about the tears in the closet, they would have been shocked. After I spoke, someone even said, "You seem so calm."

Maybe I should have just come out with it and said, "I'm having a hard time here." That's probably what I would do now. But back then I was still in the mode of trying hard and keeping it together and pushing through.

I needed someone to somehow see the truth and know I was not okay. I wanted someone to come for me and remind me I was loved and my worth didn't depend on my work. I hoped someone would rescue me. And Someone did.

When we think of Jesus as the Shepherd seeking us, we tend to focus on those times we've wandered far away. We know he carries home the rebels and corrals the lost and searches for the drifters. But there is another time when sheep need their Shepherd to come for them too. In the words of modern shepherd Chuck Wooster,

> Sheep go out of their way to disguise when they are sick or in distress. . . . Sheep will go to great lengths to appear inconspicuous when they are in trouble. Therefore, the first place to look for a sick sheep is not right in front of you—waving its hooves up and down, trying to get your attention —but deep in the middle of your flock, trying to look invisible.[1]

Jesus sees through our facades to the places where we're sick and hurt and broken. I've always wondered why Psalm 23 says, "He makes me lie down in green pastures" (Ps. 23:2). Why would anyone need to make a sheep lie down? I'm up for a nap anytime. But it turns out sheep won't lie down when they're afraid. I picture a sheep that looks a lot like me standing there saying, "I'm fine," while her knees knock and her heart pounds. Maybe what we really need is to lie down on the inside, to not be so strong all the time, to receive the care we need.

That's what Jesus brought me that weekend at the retreat. He found me when it didn't look to anyone else like I'd gone missing. He whispered the truth my heart longed for as I stood in front of a crowd again and wondered how to love them well. He refreshed my soul when I felt overwhelmed by insecurity and inadequacy.

The times when we look the most put together might actually be the ones when we're falling apart. Our Good Shepherd knows this. Because he really, truly knows us.

Shepherd,

it's beautiful that you know me so well. You see my heart and what I truly feel even when it may seem like I'm fine on the outside. Here's how I'm really doing and what I need today:
_____. *Amen.*

THIRTEEN

Comforter

> Praise be to the God and Father of our Lord
> Jesus Christ, the Father of compassion and the
> God of all comfort, who comforts us in all our
> troubles.
>
> 2 Corinthians 1:3–4

The farmers market is crowded this morning. Vegetables in every color are laid out across tables like squares on patchwork quilts. Dogs on leashes strain toward each other or the enticing hydrant on the corner. Babies bask in strollers with dribbles down their chubby chins. Toddlers place one hand in Mama's and wrap the other around organic all-fruit Popsicles.

Oh dear, there it is. The weekly tragedy. A grip loosened in a moment of forgetfulness or exuberance and that Popsicle falling down, down, down to land with a splat on the sizzling pavement.

Then the tears come, an instant river, followed by the snot and the hollering. Mama leans down, and of course, she says, "Knock it off, kid. You want to know about loss? Yesterday the stock market dropped a bazillion points. An earthquake wiped out a city. The manager at your dad's office just ran off with the intern. Again. Let's put this in perspective."

No? You don't like that version of the story? Then how about this one: Mama leans in and speaks soothing words until that river dries up, the nose is not so pink, and the only sounds are a slight sniffling. She speaks until the little head nods and the smile returns and the hand is taken again. Then the two go off in search of another Popsicle, or perhaps something even better.

Sometimes it is more complicated than this. Sometimes it is harder and takes longer. But this is the actual plotline I've been audience to again and again. This makes sense to us, and even if it's not what we've personally experienced, it's what seems right to us—that a parent would comfort a child even over the little things.

Yet I will confess I've often not expected God to treat me this way. I've been hurt or faced a loss or found fear catching me by surprise and I've told myself, "This is too insignificant to bother God about. It's nothing compared to what other people face." Then I think of the news headline, the social media post, or the prayer request, and I tell myself I'm selfish for even thinking I have a right to mourn the silly "dropped Popsicle" that's spreading a purple stain on the ground of my day.

But God says he will comfort us "in *all* our troubles" (2 Cor. 1:4, emphasis added). There is no size limit. No height requirement. No difficulty level assigned. It's unequivocal, universal, all-encompassing. The other day my daughter called and shared a hard thing. Then she said, "I'm sorry for bothering you with something so small." And I said, "If it matters to you, it matters to me."

I thought afterward, with a bit of surprise, that this must be how the heart of our God is toward us. He is not waiting for us to get over it, to snap out of it and put on a brave face. He is instead coming for us with outstretched arms to wipe the tears from our cheeks, to pull us close, to whisper love words until we are ready to take his hand again.

Yes, we need to know nothing is too big for our God to handle. But we also need to know nothing is too small for him to reach out his hands to us and hold us close.

Comforter,
it means so much to know you care
about every detail of my life. Today
I'm struggling with _____.
Thank you for listening, responding, and
walking through this with me. Amen.

FOURTEEN

Encourager

You, LORD, hear the desire of the afflicted;
you encourage them, and you listen to
their cry.

Psalm 10:17

I'm sitting next to a window at the front of a little café this morning. A few minutes ago, the skies split open and began pouring buckets of water down toward the earth. I look at a spindly potted plant with its leaves stretched up a trellis as if reaching out to catch every drop. I can almost hear it sigh with relief because of the respite from the summer heat and dryness.

I imagine those trickles making their way into the soil, going down to the roots, where they'll be part of the growth and life that's coming. I think, in many ways, this is how encouragement works. It's the words and acts that seep into our hearts. *Encouragement* means to give support, confidence, or hope to someone. Without it we begin to feel dry, our insides dusty and silent.

I found myself in such a place just yesterday. I'm in the middle of a season of serving in many ways through writing, counseling some friends going through hard times, and just the busyness of every-day, messy life. Without even fully realizing it, I began to pray, "Lord, will you please send someone to encourage me?" It felt like an odd thing to ask for, but I let the request hang in the air, suspended, and then went about my day.

Hours later I got a voice message on my phone. A dear friend said, "God put you on my heart and I felt like I was supposed to tell you . . ." and she went on with the kindest encouragement. I cried a little. Just as a disclaimer, there have been many other times I've prayed for encouragement and the response has not been this direct or clear. But for some reason, on this occasion, God decided to let me see the connection directly. And in doing so, I could also see the real Encourager behind this exchange. It was my friend's voice, but it was my heavenly Father's heart.

God is our encourager. Jesus is our encourager. The Holy Spirit is our encourager. This is a mysterious and beautiful reality to me. To think that the One who spoke the world into being would also speak into my life. To dare to believe that the One who gave his life for me also breathes life into my tired bones. To understand that the One who counts every hair on my head also addresses every care in my heart.

When we wonder, *How is God encouraging me today?* I think we can look several places. First, his Word is one long love letter of encouragement. Also, God encourages us through each other like my friend did. In this broken world, we are the hands and feet and care of God to each other. We can even encourage ourselves. "David encouraged himself in the LORD his God" (1 Sam. 30:6 KJV).

Wherever our encouragement comes from, the ultimate source is the One who loves us. Whenever we need it, he pours it out like rain for our parched hearts, like water for our weary souls. He promises to give us what we need to persevere and grow.

Encourager,
thank you so much for all you pour into
me. Help me see your hand and heart
in every word and act that builds me
up and gives me strength. Please use
me to encourage others too. Amen.

FIFTEEN

All-sufficient

And God is able to bless you abundantly, so
that in all things at all times, having all that
you need, you will abound in every good work.

2 Corinthians 9:8

I grip the steering wheel, grit my teeth, and slam
my foot on the gas pedal. My car moves forward,
but I stay stuck inside. Old worries, fears, and lies
feel like chains around my ankles today. I tug and
twist, try to pick the lock, and then finally surrender. "God," I pray, "I need you to remind me

of what's true right now. Will you set me free all over again?"

At the heart of what I'm struggling against is this: a belief that everything depends on me. I must perform. I must deliver. I must not let anyone down. In other words, God has a plan for my life, but I'd better hustle to make it happen. On the outside, these beliefs can lead to what looks like a lot of good things. I'm responsible. I work hard. I hit deadlines. But on the inside I can be hurting, afraid, and worn out.

Maybe you've been there too. If so, there's a truth we can remember together: *God is all-sufficient.* This means that because he lives in us, we have everything we need to fulfill his purpose for our lives. And the really miraculous part is that he will do it. The beginning, the middle, and the end do not depend on us. They all depend on him.

Ephesians 2:10 says, "We are God's handiwork, created in Christ Jesus to do good works, which God prepared in advance for us to do." In other words, God isn't saying, "Do as much as you can, as quickly as you can, however you can." Instead, he has specific assignments for us during our time on earth. They are not the same as the ones he has for the woman we admire, the friend we respect, or the leader we want to emulate. They are original and only for us.

What we're to do not only begins with God; it is finished by him too. "He who began a good work in you will carry it on to completion until the day of Christ Jesus" (Phil. 1:6). He does this "in all things at all times" (2 Cor. 9:8).

What's our part in all of this? We can focus on, as Jesus said, remaining close to him. We can abide, love, and obey rather than strive, hustle, and prove our value. We can rest, receive, and trust that our worth doesn't come from our works. We can release comparison and instead embrace what God has for us, believing it is enough and even beautiful in his eyes.

As I write these words, I can feel a sigh of relief inside. I can hear the snap of a chain and a clink as it falls to the ground. I can sense my soul moving forward, free again. I relax my grip on the steering wheel, let my jaw loosen, and ease up on the gas pedal. I fix my eyes on the horizon and follow the road. I'll let the car get me where I need to go and maybe even dare to enjoy the ride.

All-sufficient God,

*you are enough for all that's in front
of me. I trust you and believe you will
see me through. I especially need you to
_____ today.
I love you and choose to abide in you. Amen.*

SIXTEEN

Keeper

Whoever comes to me I will never drive away.

John 6:37

I scoot a desk out of a corner and down the hall-way. It's nothing fancy, black painted pressboard with little wooden pegs holding it together. We built it from pieces that came in a box, and I'm moving it from our guest room, which is currently our daughter's bedroom, to a new location. Lovelle isn't using it, and I'm in need of a writing spot. I set my laptop on it and don't give it another thought.

I hear Lovelle come home after a date with her fiancé later that night. The bedroom door opens with a swish across the carpet and then there is an unfamiliar pause—she is always going, always moving. I note it but sleep comes and my eyelids close.

The next morning, she is wary, circling the kitchen like it's made of eggshells and glass. Finally, I raise an eyebrow. "What's going on?" I ask. She looks at me, uncertain, and says, "You moved the desk." I consider this, confused. "Yes, you weren't using it, and I needed another place to write. It's in the other room. I'll put it back if you'd like." She exhales then, a great relief that begins in her chest, then travels up through her shoulders and into her face. "I thought you were kicking me out," she whispers.

I am stunned and silent for a long second as I look at this girl I love, who I had waited for, who I would lay down my very life for if it came down to it. "I don't understand," I say, "but I want to." She goes on, "When I lived in foster homes and other places, sometimes that would happen. They'd start giving me signals like moving things out of my room and then they would say I'd have to go." I hate this for her immediately and down to my very bones.

I try to wrap my mind around what she had imagined last night. Did she picture us removing the furniture from her room bit by bit? First the little desk, then the big bookshelves, and finally the just-right bed, until we simply said, "Oops, I guess there's no place for you here."

I come to her, put my arms around her. "I'm so sorry. I didn't know it would make you feel that way to move the desk. If I had, I never would have done it. We are never going to kick you out. We are never going to leave you. We are here for you always." She nods, tears coming, and we stand there for a moment, suspended between grace and the gurgling coffeepot on the kitchen counter.

I think of this later as the day unfolds and, of course, doesn't go as planned. I mess up. I fall short. I am aware of my own inadequacy. I begin looking around my heart to see if God has noticed. And, if so, what will he do? Will he take away his blessings? Drag them to the dumpster when I'm not looking? Maybe I'll no longer have his favor or his kindness. Or even his love. He'll dismantle the home of my heart bit by bit until at last he tells me, "It's time for you to go." Then he'll walk me to the front door and say, "You tried hard, but it just didn't work out."

This is what the enemy—sneaky trickster and liar and abandoner, accuser and false evictor—would have me believe.

I am not so different from my daughter. God has promised to keep me. Yet I sometimes act as if I'm just a guest on probation, passing through, and eventually my time will be up because I can't meet all the expectations and requirements.

But it is not so. "Whoever comes to me I will *never* drive away" (John 6:37, emphasis added). And *"Never* will I leave you; *never* will I forsake you" (Heb. 13:5). Never, never, never. This sounds like a reassuring parent whispering in the dark to a worried child being tucked in at bedtime. No exceptions. No conditions. No "We'll see how you do and then decide."

We are God's, always and always. We have a home with him, in him. We do not have to fear. The incident with the desk happened years ago, and I am still discovering, along with my daughter, what love really means. It's more than a feeling or sentiment. It's not just a temporary promise, not a poem in pencil or a cheap jukebox song. It's a place where we belong.

We live in love.

And love lives in us.

Keeper,
you are the place we can fully be safe.
You will never leave me. You will never
let me go. You will never tell me to move
on to somewhere new because I have let
you down or disappointed you. Help my
heart to fully believe that's true. Amen.

SEVENTEEN

Dwelling Place

Lord, you have been our dwelling place
throughout all generations.

Psalm 90:1

The plane touches the ground and I unbuckle my
seat belt, practically leaping into the aisle as soon
as the flight attendant allows it. An empty packet
of peanuts crackles in my pocket and my worn-
around-the-edges black suitcase follows behind
me like a loyal mutt. This marks the end of a mara-
thon of travel in my life—twenty trips in twelve
months—and I can't wait to get home.

This happened some time ago now, but that feeling is still fresh in my mind. I think of it as I sit on the back porch of my home, watching the squirrels play tag like kids at recess. I recall it when my husband reaches out to take my hand as we sit on the couch. I remember when I lay my head on a pillow at night that has grooves and curves that fit only me. In those moments, a deep contentment sweeps over me.

It's what was missing in the airports and hotels and noisy restaurants. I would find myself at extraordinary places with wonderful people, but in many ways I wasn't really there. I was homesick on the inside for the familiar and the ordinary. For the place I really belonged.

I fought this for a long time. I wanted to be the kind of person who could go and go and go. Send me across the globe. Give me a seat on that bus. Let me set my alarm to another time zone. But I am finding, especially as more years slip by, that all of us—even the most adventurous—have a longing for a place to dwell.

During that busy, busy year, I think what truly wore me out was not the traveling my body did but the internal hopping I did from one place to another. The traveling was only a symptom of another kind of restlessness. One day my identity would be located in my work. The next it would be in my ability to please an audience. Then it would be floating somewhere around the internet. My security was here, there, everywhere. And this made me feel weary, like I had inner jet lag I just couldn't get over. I felt lost and confused. So I just kept searching, kept thinking the next place would be the one where my insecurity couldn't follow me.

I did this until I just couldn't carry on anymore. Then God gathered me up in his arms and carried me back to where I belonged. Before this season in my life I hadn't really grasped what God meant when he said in Scripture, "I will be your Dwelling Place." But I slowly came to understand these words mean he will be the place where we can put down roots and make a homestead like a pioneer and claim the land as ours forever. No one will be able to kick us out or run us off or encroach on what's ours.

It turns out our heart-home is not one with walls and ceilings and two and a half bathrooms. It's God himself, our maker and caretaker and the One who knows us best of all. When we center ourselves in him, when we plant ourselves right in the middle of his will, then we are always safe and where we belong. We can remain or go. We can move or be still. We can venture or nest.

This is what I needed to know when I was a wanderer. It's the truth I am holding on to here and now, the one I'll take with me if I get on another plane: home is not a place; home is a Person. And he is with us always. His love is the place we can stay wherever we go.

Dwelling Place,
you are my security and my identity. You
are the home of my heart. You are where I
belong. Help me remain in you wherever
I go and whatever I do today. Amen.

EIGHTEEN

Confidence

For you have been my hope, Sovereign
Lord,
my confidence since my youth.

Psalm 71:5

"I just know you're going to have a baby," the
woman declares as she places her hand on my
shoulder. She's approached me after an event and
I recognize the look in her eyes. It's sincere and
kind. She's heard or read part of the story of my
infertility and she wants to make it hurt less. She's
trying to comfort me the best way she knows how.

During the almost ten years my husband and
I walked the journey of infertility, I had many en-
counters like this one. I appreciated that others

wanted to encourage me, but I had a nagging sense that God's plan for us might not align with these proclamations. I worried that I was doubting. I wrestled a lot with what faith really means. Is it believing in a particular outcome? Is it telling ourselves that we'll get what we want?

Hebrews 11:1 says, "Now faith is confidence in what we hope for and assurance about what we do not see." If we take these words at face value, then we could assume that faith is just the more spiritual version of a wish. We picture what we long for and then hold on to that vision come what may.

But if this is so, then it sounds like it might all depend on us. It's about the effort we put into believing. It's about being good enough to have what we pray for granted. This seems to me to be a recipe for disappointment and bitterness, shame and guilt. Because if we must make it happen and then it doesn't, surely it means we must have done something wrong.

I've been tempted to go down this path many times. When month after month brings heartbreak, you become desperate and wild to have a little control. You want the secret formula that will make the pain go away, that will ensure you get your way.

But what I really wanted, even more than a baby, was to know I would be okay no matter what. That I was loved and held and Someone greater than me still spun the earth. I understood that underneath all my pretty prayers and right answers I was still human and my shoulders could not bear the weight of my future.

So when I read David's words—"You have been my hope, Sovereign LORD, my confidence since my youth" (Ps. 71:5)—it felt like finding the key to a locked door, the back entrance to the place my heart had been longing for all along. Because those words mean this: when Hebrews says, "Faith is confidence," it's not saying to trust in a particular outcome. It's telling us the only sure bet is to place our faith in God himself. It means being certain he is good no matter what. He has a plan that's bigger than we can see. He loves us more than we can imagine.

When I began to embrace that reality, my anxiety and fear started to subside. Yes, I still experienced grief. But I did not feel so weighed down and alone. Over time, God began to shift my expectations and demands. So when he brought us a twenty-year-old to adopt instead of giving us a baby, we were ready. Our daughter, Lovelle, is a gift better than I could have dreamed up.

I am learning faith is not about what we want to happen; it's about Who we're trusting in no matter what the future holds. God is our hope. He is our confidence. He is the answer to every question, longing, and whispered, uncertain prayer.

Confidence,

*you are the One I place my trust in, who will
not let me down or let me go, who is working
out a plan beyond what I can even imagine.
I choose to release my expectations and
instead embrace what is unchanging—who
you are and your eternal love for me. Amen.*

NINETEEN

Tear-Catcher

You number my wanderings;
Put my tears into Your bottle;
Are they not in Your book?

Psalm 56:8 NKJV

She holds a bottle up to the light. It's small, only an inch or two high, and the deepest, most brilliant cobalt blue. It's decorated with silver like a miniature treasure—something someone might wrap in a handkerchief and tuck away in the corner of a drawer where no one can see, or set on the shelf of a china hutch where everyone can. It's mysterious, this vessel, and I can't figure out its purpose. Is it holding perfume that smells like ancient exotic flowers? Is it a fancy shaker to stash in your purse so you can sprinkle salt over French fries?

Then author and speaker Sheila Walsh begins to explain from the stage of the Designed for Life conference that this little bottle has one singular and sacred destiny: it is a tear-catcher. A friend of hers discovered it in an antique shop in Israel. Sheila says, "I did a little research and discovered that tear bottles were common in Rome and Egypt around the time of Christ. Mourners would collect their tears as they walked toward the graveyard to bury their loved one, a tangible indication of how much that person was loved."[1]

Suddenly Psalm 56:8 shifts like a kaleidoscope and I can see it from a new perspective. Human mourners walked and caught their *own* tears. But our wild God takes it one step further: he catches *our* tears and walks beside us in *our* sorrows. This changes everything. Because if we are carrying our own bottle of tears, then we are spilling our sadness only into emptiness. But if God is beside us, if those tears are going into his bottle, then we are releasing them into the hands of One who can not only hold them but also transform them. "Weeping may stay for the night, but rejoicing comes in the morning" (Ps. 30:5). He can take what seems hopeless and turn it into victory. He can make beauty out of brokenness. He can redeem and restore anything.

Sheila Walsh has known this firsthand. Through dark nights of depression, valleys of anxiety, and thoughts of drying up those tears completely by ending it all. But now she stands firm on the stage in front of me, little bottle in her hand, and invites women who are hurting to come to the front of the room. And they do. Teenagers with pink-streaked hair, weary mamas with spit-up stains on their shirts, and grandmothers crowned with silver. They are mourners in the aisles this morning. Hands grasped, hearts bared, and heads bowed.

The woman in front of me lets go of a single tear and I see it, suspended in midair for a second, before it disappears. I imagine it sliding into the tear-catcher, held by an unseen hand. The place where it can be more than salt and water, where it can be a secret ingredient in the kind of miracle God makes out of the most unexpected moments of our lives. We can be certain of this: nothing, not even one drop, is ever overlooked or wasted with him.

Tear-Catcher,

*you are the One who knows every sorrow
I've experienced and every struggle I've faced.
You've caught my tears of hurt, frustration,
and grief. Thank you for treasuring all
of them and transforming them into
something new and beautiful. Amen.*

TWENTY

Truth

Jesus answered, "I am the way and the truth
and the life."

John 14:6

Wheels whir along the road, and words inside our
car move just as fast. My dear friend and I talk and
laugh, catching up on everything from our latest
haircuts to the hardest moments of our weeks.
We're on a road trip with our husbands—a time to
get away and eat too many snacks. I'm in desperate
need of this and my friend knows it.

At a certain point in the conversation, she turns
to her bag and pulls out a journal. It's worn with

the touch of fingertips and there's ink smudged across the edges of the pages. She finds the spot she's looking for and I see my name in her handwriting. She clears her throat and begins to tell me what she's been praying over my life, intentionally and fervently. She says she has some questions for me, and I nod for her to continue. She asks me about my full calendar and empty tank. She inquires about why I've said yes to certain requests that don't seem to fit with who I am. She wants to understand why I feel compelled to run at such a hectic pace lately, a blur of stress and striving.

I blink back tears and at first she misunderstands. She thinks she's hurt me and she's worried. But the opposite is true. I feel so loved. I feel seen. I feel worth fighting for because she was brave enough to say these hard things, to ask these tough questions. She has looked past my smile and my "I'm fine" and my performance. Instead of applauding my efforts, as many people seem to, she has put a hand on my shoulder and looked into my eyes, my heart. She has given me what I wanted most but didn't know how to ask for, which was for someone to help me pause and remember that I don't have to do all this to be loved.

This happened years ago, but when I think of what truth really means, I still go back to that moment. Folks have pointed out things in my life at other times. But I have felt the harshness underlying the sugary words, the sting of judgment, or the smack of expectations. What they said might have been factually true, but it wasn't coming from a place of love, and my heart just couldn't receive it. But not this time, not with this friend.

I realized, because of her, what Jesus really means when he tells us he is truth. He is not waiting to give us a list of our wrongs. He is not recounting our character flaws. He is not reminding us of why we don't measure up. Instead, he is "speaking the truth in love," as he calls us to do (Eph. 4:15). He is saying, "I love you. I see you. I care what's going on in your heart and life. I know who you really are. This is what you need to know so that you can be whole."

I think sometimes we get confused. We read about "the sword of the Spirit, which is the word of God" (Eph. 6:17), and we think this means we are to go around swinging that sword at each other. But truth is always and only to defend the people we love. To protect each other's hearts. To say, "I see a threat in your life, and I am willing to put myself on the line on your behalf."

This is what my friend did in a car on a road trip. This is what Jesus did on a cross and when he came forth from an empty tomb. This is what we can dare to do for each other.

Truth is more than facts or opinions. Truth is a Person who loves us. He wants to speak to our hearts today.

Truth,

you are the only One who is fully truth
and fully love. Help me remember that
and model it for others. Give me words
to speak that will truly encourage others,
and tune me in to the words you want
to share with my heart too. Amen.

TWENTY-ONE

sustainer

Surely God is my help;
    the Lord is the one who sustains me.

Psalm 54:4

I pull my journal out of the nightstand and begin to write in loopy, early morning script, my eyes still only half-open. The day before comes back to me—the intense meetings, impending deadlines, emails I've yet to answer.

True confession: my stressed-out self went not to the cross but to the kitchen. And when my husband came home, I asked if we could go on a date night. I thought this would be a magic cure—a fun evening on a patio, a cupcake for dessert, Netflix when we got home. But when my head hit the pillow, I still felt weary. And now I've woken up the same way. In the near dark it seems God whispers to my searching heart, "Will you let me be your Sustainer?"

Now I want to pause and say that food and time with those we love and relaxation are all gifts from God. He offers them to us freely and joyfully. I didn't sense that God was saying, "You shouldn't have done any of that." Rather, he was telling me, "For what you needed, those weren't enough."

I paused and wondered, *How might I have handled that hard day differently?* I think it would have simply been this: I would have invited Jesus into the kitchen with me. I would have sat at the table, and yes, I still might have had a treat, but I would have talked to him while I did so. I would have told him of my tiredness, hurt, and fear. My frustration and exhaustion. I would have let him be the one to truly fill me.

I still would have gone on my date night, but I would have given Jesus a seat at the table too. I would have shared more with my husband and asked him to pray for me. I would have gone home and watched Netflix in my pajamas, but I would have asked Jesus to wrap his love around me like the soft blanket on my couch. As I drifted off to sleep later, I would have released all my cares to him.

Sustain means "strengthen and support," and I'm learning, slowly, to lean on Jesus instead of flimsy earthly things that can never hold my weight. These are not "bad," it's simply that we sometimes ask far more of them than they are able to give. A cupcake can't heal my heart. Another episode can't give me peace. They have their place; they can contribute. We need not feel guilty for enjoying them. *But they are only nice supplements and not true sustenance.*

This is the miracle: the God of the universe, the creator of cupcakes, the spinner of the earth, and the maker of our hearts says he is our Sustainer. This can feel big and mysterious. But I think it simply comes down to inviting him into our every-day moments, letting his shoulder be the one we lean on, asking his love to be our strength and support.

I sit on the edge of my bed and whisper, "Yes, Lord, be my Sustainer today." It is a prayer he always answers, one all the stressed-out folks can say.

Sustainer,
thank you that I can come to you no matter
what I need or what kind of day I've had.
You give me so many good blessings and
you are always the very best. Help me draw
strength, hope, and joy from you. Amen.

TWENTY-TWO

Provider

My God will meet all your needs according to the riches of his glory in Christ Jesus.

Philippians 4:19

Sleep is trying to drag me back to bed like a nagging toddler while I stand at the stove over two eggs with bright yellow centers. As I wait for my breakfast to be ready, I press play on a message from a friend. I listen on speaker, her voice in my kitchen as if she's leaning against the counter next to me. We have an ongoing conversation, this friend and I, stopped and started in spare moments. In the car, the laundry room, coffee shops, and on the couch late at night. This morning she asks, "What's it like for you to be married?"

I stand, considering this question, with my hands on my hips, still in my pajamas, hair wild and eyes half-open. Perhaps it's this less-than-fully-conscious state that makes me decide to go ahead and respond rather than wait and process like I normally would. I push the little button that will send my reply to her.

I say, "What comes to mind first is that God knows what we need. He chooses for us even better than we do." I go on to share how personality tests label my husband and me "incompatible." Among other things, he's high on the practical scale and I on the emotional one. Then I add, "But Jesus . . ." He knew how the paths of our lives would go, how our stories would unfold. He gave me not what Hollywood would tell me is the only way to happily ever after but instead what's truly best.

I think then of the story of our daughter as well. Ten years of infertility led us to a twenty-year-old who had almost given up hope of finding parents. Our family is strange and wonderful and fits into the spaces of our hearts as if it was always made to be there. Because it was.

God will meet our needs "according to the riches of his glory in Christ Jesus" (Phil. 4:19). This isn't adequate; it's abundant. It's extravagant. It's limitless. Perhaps what matters even more to me is that it's *personal*. When God provides, it's not one-size-fits-all. The One who numbers every hair on our heads knows every desire in our hearts.

This doesn't mean we will get everything we request. God promises instead the only thing better than what we want—what we really need. Here's the secret: he alone knows what that is. We might articulate or calculate, list or describe. But we're still amateurs, guessing and grasping.

When I look back over the requests I've prayed and the wishes I've asked to be granted, I'm grateful that so many of them were met with a benevolent *no*. Among other things, I would have woken up every Christmas morning to a new pony, monkey, and large tortoise. All of which I had room for in my childhood imagination but not in my actual living room.

Yes, there are other prayers I still go back to and touch with confusion and tears. They will remain a mystery until eternity. With those it's a comfort to know Someone does understand. And this Someone loves me more than I can comprehend. The God who gave his Son is not holding out or holding back. He is not unfamiliar with ache and longing. He does not treat our disappointments or desires lightly.

I slide my eggs onto the plate alongside the rest of my breakfast and refill my coffee cup. I consider what's in front of me this morning. It is good. It is more than enough. I bow my head and I give thanks.

Provider,

you know not only my needs but also my
wants, desires, hopes, and longings. Thank
you for working out what is best for me even
when I don't understand. In return, I choose
to trust you and your plan today. Amen.

TWENTY-THREE

Instructor

Good and upright is the LORD;
    therefore he instructs sinners in his
      ways.
He guides the humble in what is right
    and teaches them his way.
All the ways of the LORD are loving and
      faithful
    toward those who keep the demands
      of his covenant.

                       Psalm 25:8–10

The grass is still early morning wet when we unfold the chairs we've carried here. The field in front of us is marked with white lines. In between those, children about as high as my waist run like a patch of moving wildflowers. There are crew cuts and ponytails, red uniforms and blue, socks slipping down toward ankles. We settle in and prepare to cheer. The whistle blows and the chaos begins. The object to be paid attention to in this moment is a soccer ball, and it is approached with equal parts fervency and distraction.

One girl notices a dog being walked around the perimeter by its owner. She pauses mid-kick to shout, "Mom, look at the puppy!" Someone else is temporarily transfixed by the moving clouds in the sky above. One ambitious kid intensely engages the ball with his foot and a clod of dirt goes flying, up and up, as everyone else halts to watch openmouthed. My athletically inclined nephew shakes his head. He is the goalie.

In the middle of all this is a referee. Brown-haired. Middle-aged. Bright yellow shirt. At first I don't pay much attention to him. He does what referees are supposed to, which is to let the game take its course without being a distraction. But as kids make mistakes, I begin to watch his responses. There is exuberant line-crossing, and he calmly explains what out of bounds means. A curly blond head nods. Someone snatches the ball midair and I watch the conversation, including both hand and foot motions, telling the confused player why this is not allowed. Another nod. A smile. One freckled player scrunches up her face as if to cry as soon as the whistle blows. "It's okay," he tells her. "It's okay." Then he explains what to do differently next time.

Perhaps it's this interaction that gets me most. Because I am that girl, forever kicking the ball out of bounds with the best of intentions. The one who berates herself on the inside before anyone else even has time to say a word. The one ready for the discipline and the rebuke and the shame penalty. But, instead, it's as if God, in his loving-kindness, comes over, leans down, and says to me, "It's okay. It's okay." Then he tells me how to do it differently next time. And here's the miracle: there's always a next time.

It's not as if these kids are even in utter rebellion. They are not spraying graffiti on the goalposts, tripping the other team, or stealing the sports drinks. That would have required a different response. They are simply *growing*. And this, not the little box at each end of the field, is actually the goal of the game. I think we forget this sometimes. Then when we mess up, when we are human, when we don't know better yet, we hunker down and get scared because we think a big bad God is coming for us at any second. Yes, he will come. But it will be to reassure and instruct and help us learn. He is patient, so patient.

Eventually the game wraps up and the little players dash to the edges of the field. "Well done," they are told. The witnesses waiting in lawn chairs affirm, hug, and pat backs. I watch the referee walk off the field too. Along the way he tousles the hair of a child standing on the sidelines. "Well done," he says. "Good game."

Instructor,
thank you for being so gentle, kind, and
patient with me. I am so grateful you see
beyond my mistakes and to my heart. You
love me as I am today and you help me
learn and grow for tomorrow. Amen.

TWENTY-FOUR

Holy-Maker

We have been made holy through the sacrifice
of the body of Jesus Christ once for all.

Hebrews 10:10

I step up to the counter. The barista has black hair, a braided flock of ravens down her back. She is pierced and smiling in a shirt the color of a burgundy autumn leaf. She asks what I'd like. There are so many ways to answer, but I stick to the coffee: twelve-ounce almond milk latte. My go-to drink, my security blanket in a cardboard cup that I will clutch until the last drop is gone and I must, reluctantly, set it down. She spins around the fancy screen that says your order and lets you sign for it. When she does, she laughs and says, "I forgot the extra *l* in your name."

She's actually forgotten the *e* too, so what I see in a flashing second is "Holy." I want to blush and hide and call it a lie. I think of the sharp-pointed words I waved around like a fork at breakfast. I imagine the moment of worry in the car when I let my thoughts spin their wheels toward what-ifs like an out-of-control semitruck. I am quick to recall the verse I read propped up in bed and how I have already shredded it with my imperfect little fingers into a million confetti pieces. It's only 9:00 a.m.

And yet I also realize in that moment that this is not the only time I have been called *holy*. God has done it too: "We have been made holy through the sacrifice of the body of Jesus Christ once for all" (Heb. 10:10). This is strange and mysterious and a bit scandalous. Like calling a pauper the queen or the freckled mutt the champion of the ritzy dog show. It's startling and unnerving. It's comforting and inspiring. It's something only our Grace-Giver would do.

As long as we're here on earth, we're still in the process of conforming to what we already are. We don't always *act* holy. But we still *are* holy because of what Jesus has done for us.

The barista notes the three seconds of quiet and the furrowed brow. She says, "Oh, don't worry, we won't call your name out that way!" We both grin a bit at the thought of an entire coffee shop turning to see who's answering to the shout of "Holy!"

I have been known to answer to lesser names, to "not good enough" and "disappointment" and "unloved." These are hollered by the enemy of my soul, the one who would trap and diminish me. But when we are following Jesus, we don't need to pay this any mind. God "has reconciled you by Christ's physical body through death to present you holy in his sight, without blemish and free from accusation" (Col. 1:22).

It's that last part that gets me most: *free from accusation*. In other words, there is no name-calling allowed on God's playground. There is only renaming. Chosen, accepted, beloved, forgiven, and more, strung together like a proclamation. And yes, "holy" is part of it too.

I find a table and a few minutes later I hear it: "Holley!" I go to what's mine and take hold of it. No one else has heard the previous exchange with the barista. It's evaporated into the espresso-scented air, hovering invisibly somewhere nearby. As I take my seat, I think, *I know the truth. I know the whole story.*

I am talking about more than the coffee now: I am claiming and declaring and thanking the God who reminds us of who we really are.

Holy-Maker,
thank you for purifying my heart in
ways that are deeper than I can see
or imagine. Thank you for calling me
who I really am in you and freeing me
from accusation. Help me to listen to
your voice above all others. Amen.

TWENTY-FIVE

Deliverer

The Lord is my rock, my fortress and my deliverer.

2 Samuel 22:2

The door opens and the scent of chili simmering on the stove grabs me like an eager hostess. It's warm, spicy, an invitation and a bit of a challenge. This seems right for such a night. My husband and I are at a new small group for the first time, and I am nervous. I fiddle with the bracelet on my wrist like a junior high girl would, as if it has magic somewhere under the gold. I want it to make these people like me, blind them to the dark roots in my hair, close their ears to my awkward small talk, make them smile and nod and ask, "Will you be my friend?"

We sit and they are kind. I breathe a sigh of relief and pick up my spoon. There's yellow cornbread, butter, cranberries, and apple pie. There's the clanking of silverware and the clink of ice in glasses and the lilt of conversation, a bit of laughter.

After dinner we sit in a circle on couches and chairs in the living room. We lay out Bibles on our laps like fat soft-skinned babies. We read in Mark about a man that evil has a hold on in such a way that he can only live in the tombs outside town. No one can keep him chained, but he is all bound up inside. Then Jesus comes for him, takes a boat right across the water with his disciples. He goes to the one who is an outcast and casts out the demons within him.

But what impacts me even more, what I can't stop thinking about, is what happens after the man has been freed. He wants to go with Jesus. This is the answer: "Go home to your own people and tell them how much the Lord has done for you, and how he has had mercy on you" (Mark 5:19). Five minutes before, this man had been a spokesperson for all that's sinister and dark. His life is a wreck. He seems beyond redemption or rescue. And now, immediately, Jesus is saying, "I trust you to speak for me. I want you to represent me. I have a divine purpose for you."

I might have protested. I might have said, "I need more time to get ready. I need to go to seminary. I need to listen to more sermons. I need to attend some conferences or read a hundred books or have a dozen mentors." But Jesus has only one requirement for being in his service: a willingness to speak the truth of our deliverance. Not the cleaned-up, edited, and polished version. No, the one with the part about how we are living right in the middle of death and then there is life. How we drive everyone we love away and then love comes for us anyway. The one where we are the villain until someone sees more than that in us and gives us the mission of a hero.

We are all this man. Because this story is a preview of the resurrection. Jesus came for us. He braved the tombs. He released us. He sent us out.

And now it is our turn to decide what we will do about it. Will we dare to believe we can be of use as we are, even with our pasts, our messes, our mistakes?

I'm glad I decided to show up "as is" this evening. And this is what our little group suddenly knows in a living room with the scent of chili still in the air: it's not the wise God wants but the willing. Not the faultless but the faithful. We don't need a permission slip, a résumé, a squeaky-clean record, or a degree—we only need a story about a God who loves us and sets us free. And we all have one.

Deliverer,

you have done for me what I could never do for myself. You have brought me out of darkness and into the light. You have rescued me and set me free. I ask that you would give me opportunities to tell of your love, grace, and power today. Amen.

TWENTY-SIX

Refuge

Trust in him at all times, you people;
pour out your hearts to him,
for God is our refuge.

Psalm 62:8

I take a seat in the coffee shop at a long wood table, scarred and rough-edged. It's known the days and nights, the conversations and silences, the sear of a hot cup and the rub of a thousand hands. I feel a companionship with it this morning and try to set my computer gently upon it.

In front of me are two men. One is broad-shouldered and wearing a suit on an ordinary Thursday morning. The suit is stretched taut against his back, seams as if they might snap. The other man is spectacled and talks with his hands, lines on his face like a map of rivers. I discern they are pastors, and as I type they cover theology and politics, church business and ancient truths. I pay them little mind until the spectacled one grows loud. He is insisting on something, repeating it like the pound of a hammer.

"Your feelings don't matter. You have to go back to the facts." And I am the one who feels the blow, who feels like the little girl in the pew again, clutching the hymnal, wide-eyed at the man behind the pulpit. The one swallowing the lump in her throat on so many Sundays. And on the weekdays when words from a friend at the junior high lunch table sting. When her heart is broken. When a dream disappoints. When someone she loves is growing cold in the ground. It is there, always, this: "Your feelings don't matter. You have to go back to the facts."

He is talking about losing his wife. He is saying he must remember she is with Jesus. And I want to go over to him and shake him. I want to hand him a tissue and put his head on my shoulder like he's three years old. I want to tell him to cry until someone has to bring a mop because of the slick puddles. "You're wrong," I want to say to him. "Perhaps well-intentioned but so very wrong."

Because we have a God who calls himself our Refuge. And a refuge is where we are to go back to, especially when we're hurt or afraid. This is what I know: our Refuge wept at the tomb of a friend. He took a nap on a boat. He tossed the tables of money changers in frustration. He hurt and ached and smiled and laughed. He understands still what it is to be human. Even more, we are made in the image of God and we are created with emotions. So to say faith is only about facts is to amputate the heart of God in our lives. We can never experience the fullness of who he is without embracing the fullness of who we are, of this wild and vivid experience of earth living.

While facts can provide security and certainly have their place, they are also cold-edged and hard. To seek comfort in them is like sleeping on the pavement. But Jesus is open-armed and grace-filled. He is fierce in his love and mighty in his comfort. "Pour out your hearts to him, for God is our refuge" (Ps. 62:8). This is the invitation. To bring not our high-minded thoughts but our rawness and weeping, our humanity and brokenness, our soft and tender places.

The pastors are standing now. They are picking up neatly lined pads of paper. There's an orderly file under one arm, a thin white envelope in a hand. I think of the widower going home to the old house, to the echo in the halls and the empty chair at the table. I hope one day he will look up and realize Jesus is sitting there, just waiting for him to put aside the facts like an old newspaper.

I do not want to go back to the facts; I want only and always to go back to Jesus.

Refuge,

you are so tender with my heart. Thank you not only for creating me with emotions but also for fully experiencing all of them in a human way while you were on earth. You really do understand, and you are the safe place I can always go back to. Amen.

TWENTY-SEVEN

Grower

> So neither the one who plants nor the one
> who waters is anything, but only God, who
> makes things grow.
>
> 1 Corinthians 3:7

I spread the cards out like a dealer at a Las Vegas casino. "Pick a card, any card," I say to Mark. He raises his eyebrows and reaches out to take one. Fortunately, these cards aren't actually a gamble; there's no ace of spades or queen of diamonds. Instead, Mark is holding a simple white note-card with messy handwriting in black ink on one side. I've been writing down a name of God every morning along with a Scripture to go with it and have slowly built up a substantial stack. Mark has chosen "Grower: So neither the one who plants nor the one who waters is anything, but only God, who makes things grow" (1 Cor. 3:7).

He smiles and says, "Of all the cards I could have picked . . ." He doesn't even need to finish the sentence. In the shorthand that couples who have been married for a while speak, I know what he's saying. We need God to be this to us now. We're in the midst of a growing season—new business opportunities for Mark, launching a book for me, welcoming a grandbaby for both of us.

It's so easy in seasons like this one to start be-lieving it all depends on us. Perhaps you've expe-rienced this too. You look at your children and think, *I have to make sure they grow up to follow God.* You look at your work and whisper, "I have to make sure it grows into a success." You look at the dream waiting like an egg in the nest of your heart and tell yourself, "I have to make sure it grows wings."

But the reality is that *we can't make anything grow.* This sounds so contrary to our hustle-and-strive, stress-out-and-make-it-happen culture. Yet it's a reality that can bring back our peace, slow down our breathing, and return the joy to our relationships.

Yet just because we can't make things grow doesn't mean we're supposed to hang out on the couch all day. Wise Solomon said, "Sow your seed in the morning, and at evening let your hands not be idle, for you do not know which will succeed, whether this or that, or whether both will do equally well" (Eccles. 11:6).

In other words, our role is daily obedience and God's role is results.

We spend intentional time nurturing the hearts of our children even though we can't force them to choose faith.

We do our work well and with excellence even though the outcome of the project is uncertain.

We take the next step in our dreams even when it feels hard and risky.

We can be faithful workers, loving parents, and diligent dreamers. Like farmers who plant and water, we do what's within our realm of re-sponsibility. But in the end, we leave it all in God's hands.

This makes a difference because we don't have to carry the weight of what ultimately happens. We also don't claim it as our identity. The "failure" isn't proof that we're inadequate and the praise isn't proof that we're to be worshipped. Both are too much for us to carry. Instead, we can release all the criticism and praise to God and simply do the next thing he asks. *Whew.*

And here's the promise we can cling to: "If you remain in me and I in you, you will bear much fruit" (John 15:5). There *will* be growth. It may not look like what we planned, but it will come in its season.

Mark and I bow our heads and pray. It's time to start another day.

Grower,

it's so easy to live as if everything depends on me. Thank you that instead I can fully depend on you. Help me to live in obedience today and leave the rest to you. You are the Grower. You are the Life-Giver. You are the Difference-Maker. You are working mysteriously and mightily in my life today. Amen.

TWENTY-EIGHT

Peace

And he will be called . . . Prince of Peace.

Isaiah 9:6

The lights burn low in the sanctuary and the voices rise high. They echo off rafters and doors, then flow down the walls like a flood of so many waters. I close my eyes and listen, let my thoughts drift back to a year ago.

I stood here, right in this place, and felt like a warrior who had clawed her way back to her fortress after battle. Bloodied and bruised, armor dented, sword hanging by her side. "I will keep fighting," I told myself then. "I will not give up." Then I slumped inside, spent, and begged, "Jesus, help me."

And he did. He rescued me from the depression and anxiety that threatened to tear me apart, break my heart, and turn every bit of joy into ashes with their flaming torches. They were marching, always marching toward me. In my weariness, Jesus became my strength. He delivered me again and again. With the help of a counselor and a doctor and a circle of close friends, I survived. And now, a year later, I thrived.

When the pastor spoke of peace on this night when we would light the Advent candle for it, I saw it with new eyes. A year ago I thought of peace as only tranquility. The absence of something. But now, here, I knew it as the presence of Someone.

I had also learned this: there is a kind of peace that only comes after war. I could still smell the burnt edges in the air. I could touch the scars. I could run my fingers down patches in my armor. I would not forget.

The Hebrew word for "peace" is *Shalom*. It speaks of wholeness, completeness. I understand this better now, how peace comes out of brokenness, out of emptiness, out of the dark and unexpected places. I've lived it and made it through because Jesus did too. For "the punishment that brought us peace was on him" (Isa. 53:5).

I rolled these words around in my mind again and again.

No cross, no peace.

No nails, no peace.

No crown of thorns, no peace.

I thought then of how I have sometimes treated peace lightly. Even now, even after knowing better. And I told the One who fought for it on my behalf, "Never again. I will not surrender what you have gained for me." I will not define peace as the world does, as weak or even boring, as only a whisper and never a roar.

"Let there be peace on earth," the congregation sings.

I join in on the final notes, "And let it begin with me."

Peace,

you are the One who puts me back together.
My wholeness and my completeness and
the winner of my battles. Thank you
for fighting on my behalf. I will guard
what you have gained for me. Amen.

TWENTY-NINE

Hiding Place

You are my hiding place;
  you will protect me from trouble
  and surround me with songs of
    deliverance.

Psalm 32:7

It's a gray winter day with clouds like a quilt laid over everything. I'm half awake as I slide into the driver's seat of my car to head to a local coffee shop for a morning of writing. I press play on a new podcast a friend has recommended. I hear Christy Nockels, voice like honey and light, talk about what it means to find a hiding place in God.

She shares how a friend of hers, years ago, described this place like the center of a bull's-eye.

We serve and do in the outer rings. But the center, she says, "is where we're fully known as beloved by God. Inside the bull's-eye, this is who you are. It's the place you do everything from."[1] I take a deep breath and my eyes pop open as if I've downed a shot of espresso.

Just last night I had curled under layers of covers. A comforter, blanket, another blanket. Two pillows. I had burrowed down into my bed and closed my eyes. It had been a tough day, and I thought of how modern life, especially social media, sometimes leaves me feeling overexposed. I reflected on the legacy of my grandparents who owned a small Christian bookstore in a little town, who served simply and quietly for a lifetime. I whispered a paradox prayer, "Use me. Hide me." Whether it's in our work, personal circumstances, or relationships, we all have moments of feeling overwhelmed and vulnerable.

Yet it's still hard for me to utter this short prayer, because I've always thought of hiding as somehow bad. We live in a "go out there and be bold" kind of world. But it seems a longing for hiding is built into us. We tuck our faces into the necks of our parents as babies. We play hide-and-seek with our childhood friends. As adults we hide in less conspicuous ways, behind the screen of a computer, in the bottom of a glass, underneath all that makeup. So perhaps it's not about whether we will hide but rather where and how.

And this is the beautiful reality: God himself says he will be our hiding place. He will be the retreat and the fortress and the silent space in a chaotic, busy world. Where does this mean we are hidden? In love. Because "God is love" (1 John 4:8).

Christy goes on to say, "When we hide in the place that's already been carved out for us to hide in, we emerge from that place our truest selves."[2] In other words, when we find our refuge in God, we can be who we are, do what we're called to do, live without shame and guilt and fear.

When Adam and Eve fell, they hid. God came looking for them and asked, "Where are you?" (Gen. 3:9). It seems a strange question because, as God, he already knew. Perhaps he needed to ask because *they* didn't fully realize the truth. Maybe he is asking the same of us today. *Where are you?* No matter the answer we may give—"in the middle of depression," "on the battlefield," "at the center of a stage"—he wants us to know that is not our truest, deepest location. Where we belong, where we've been all along, where we always are in some mysterious way is *in him.* Secure. Loved. Known. He is our Hiding Place; he is our heart's true home.

Hiding Place,

*no matter where I am or what I do, I
am always secure and cared for in you.
That is a mystery and miracle to me.
Help me dwell in you and believe that
no one can separate me from your love,
the place where I truly belong. Amen.*

THIRTY

King

For God is the King of all the earth;
sing to him a psalm of praise.

Psalm 47:7

I am writing this on the eve of an election before
the results are in. Before the first numbers flash
on the screen and the commentators in their suits
and skirts begin telling us what it all means. Before
there is red or blue scattered across the map.

On whatever day you might be reading it, I
imagine there is still conflict and concern when
it comes to politics. So I want to talk about what
we need to know in the middle of times that roll
like the ocean. Where scandals and cynicism are as

common as the sand on the shore. Where it seems we are picking sides and picking fights even more than picking candidates.

I am weary of it all. Perhaps you are too. And maybe, just maybe, we are a little afraid too. And this is why we think, somehow, in our weaker moments, that our hope is in a person or a party. That our future can be spelled out on a ballot. That who lives in the White House really determines the security of the foundation of our house.

Can we all take a deep breath right now and remember what's true? Remember how the future is not an outcome, not an elected official. Our future is a God who hung stars in place, who spoke the world into being, who keeps it twirling on its axis still. The One who watches a billion sparrows hatch, who knows the feathers on their wings and numbers the hairs on our heads. The One who went to a cross for us and defeated death itself when he stepped outside an empty tomb.

The hands that hold us are not the ones of the baby-kissing politicians, not the ones of those who pass the laws or make the campaign promises. No, we are in the hands of the One big enough to contain the mountains and valleys, all the maps and the globes and every country on them.

Could there be hard times ahead? Certainly. Will there be surprises and tragedies and people who fall short of what they claim to be? As long as we're on this broken earth. But do we also have every reason to hope, every reason to march toward tomorrow with courage and love? Oh, yes and yes. Always and always.

No matter what the results of this election might be, no matter what is happening in our world when your eyes land on this very sentence, God will still be in charge. He is good and wise and not startled or overwhelmed by any of it. We do not need to fear the future; we need to fear him. And not in the sense of being afraid but in the more traditional meaning of the word, which has more to do with respect and trust and awe.

This is the reality. This is the truth. This is our *hope*: no matter which leader we may have, which politician may promise or lie, which person seems to hold the power, *we will have the same King*. He is good, wise, and kind. He cannot be defeated. "Let the heavens rejoice, let the earth be glad; let them say among the nations, 'The LORD reigns!'" (1 Chron. 16:31).

King,

you are the ruler of my heart and life. You are the only One who holds all the earth in his hands. To you belong the power and glory. No matter what is going on around me, I will trust and obey you. Amen.

THIRTY-ONE

Cornerstone

So this is what the Sovereign LORD says:

"See, I lay a stone in Zion, a tested stone,
  a precious cornerstone for a sure
    foundation;
the one who relies on it
  will never be stricken with panic."

Isaiah 28:16

I stand inside the bones of a building. Wooden beams stretch over my head like a rib cage. I am close to the center, where the heart would be. I run my hands along a rough board waiting for a wall to cover it like skin. My husband and I often venture into houses that have not yet fully become homes. With his training as an architect, he can picture it all before it comes to be. "This is where they'll sleep," he'll say. "This is where they'll watch TV."

So it makes sense that he's the one I ask when I come across a word in Scripture I don't understand. I'm reading in bed and his head is already on his pillow. I nudge him anyway. "What is a cornerstone?" I know this much: it is a name for Jesus. But beyond that I'm perplexed. He props himself up on one elbow and I watch him search for the words that I, the construction amateur, will understand. "It holds the weight of the structure," he explains. "It keeps it from falling apart."

I like this, and by the light of a bedside lamp I dig further. This is what I find: "It was common in the construction of first-century buildings to lean a building into itself. This meant that one part of the structure would have a greater amount of pressure on it than the rest of the structure. . . . This became known as the cornerstone and was the one part of the building on which the rest of the structure depended absolutely."[1]

One word in that description especially calls out to me: *pressure*. I think back over my busy day.

There have been deadlines, emails, phone calls, and requests. Hurting friends to comfort, dinner to cook, and socks like a gang of feral cats in need of corralling on the laundry room floor. I have felt it all like a weight: the expectations to be so many things to so many people, to get it all done perfectly and right now. I want someone to take what I can't possibly bear.

"So this is what the Sovereign Lord says: 'See, I lay a stone in Zion, a tested stone, a precious cornerstone for a sure foundation; the one who relies on it will never be stricken with panic'" (Isa. 28:16). *Never be stricken with panic.* At first this phrase sounds strange to me, but then I realize it is the very emotion that has been just beneath the surface of my skin all day. I know what it is to have hands that shake and a heart that quakes and eyes open wide in worry.

And I am not the only one.

We all need a cornerstone. Not a vague architectural term lost mostly to history, but the One who is our living, breathing, daily reality. Sometimes, like when I wander around those half-done houses, we can't quite see what all this means. But God always does, and he will remind us that "in him all things hold together" (Col. 1:17). On him all things depend. We can rest on this truth, this promise. We don't have to carry the weight of this world—or even just our little lives. We only need to keep leaning into love.

Cornerstone,

thank you for being sure, strong, and true in a world that can seem uncertain and chaotic. When I try to put pressure on myself or those around me, help me depend on you instead. Thank you for bearing the weight and holding everything together so I don't have to. I can live in freedom and grace. Amen.

THIRTY-TWO

Carpenter

> "Isn't this the carpenter? Isn't this Mary's son and the brother of James, Joseph, Judas and Simon? Aren't his sisters here with us?" And they took offense at him.
>
> Mark 6:3

Jesus knew ordinary. He knew the feel of a splinter in his thumb, the smell of earth and sawdust, the sounds of nails against boards. He understood deadlines and demanding customers. He comprehended the common, the kind of day that slips right by without fanfare or fireworks. "As carpenters, Joseph and Jesus would have created mainly farm tools (carts, plows, winnowing forks, and yokes), house parts (doors, frames, posts, and beams), furniture, and kitchen utensils."[1]

These seem like odd tasks for the Son of God. The One who sculpted the universe bending over a workbench to shape a spoon that will stir soup. The One who gave the wild sea its borders smoothing the edges of a doorframe. The One who would stretch out on a beam to save the world placing a not-so-different board beneath a faltering roof. Jesus likely would have begun his work as a carpenter while still a teenager. When we consider this, it seems a decade or more of his time on earth could have been used differently. Only 10 percent of Jesus's life was spent in public ministry.

I think we need to know this because we will all have "carpenter years." Times when we don't feel like we're living up to our potential. We feel like we could be doing something more, something bigger. We can resist the smallness. We, like the questioning crowd around Jesus, can become disappointed and disillusioned by what doesn't seem as grand as we'd imagined.

A counseling client of mine once cleared her throat and quietly asked, "What do you do if you feel like you've wasted your life?" The silence hung thick in the air between us. It's a heavy question of the heart. And I thought then too of the One who had the most meaningful existence ever. Yet for so many years, he was simply a carpenter. I say this out loud, pondering. "He didn't need more practice," I say. "And it sure seems like he could have started his ministry earlier and gotten more done. But for some inexplicable reason, he spent years working with wood. Years we would have called wasted."

She looks up, smiles. We part ways. Next time I see her she holds a sheet of paper in her hand. It has these words on it. I ask her if I can share them with you. She says yes.

Why did he need to be a Carpenter? Maybe, just maybe, he was a carpenter for me. . . . Each hurt is a board, each disappointment a piece of wood, and each trial a plank.

Jesus, the Carpenter, is taking each piece of wood and nailing it together. He is nailing together a future that is unclear to me, but I have peace because he is my Carpenter. I take great comfort in Ephesians 2:10. "For we are God's workmanship created in Christ Jesus to do good works, which God prepared in advance for us to do."

I understand that my past was not wasted. He is using it all to "build" me so I can do the good works God has prepared for me to do. I don't know what he has in store for me in the next phase of my life; however, it doesn't matter, because he is building me into his Masterpiece.[2]

Is this why Jesus spent all those years as a carpenter? I think it's likely one reason of many. So much of God's plan is a mystery. But those "wasted" years in his life, in ours? It seems clear there is no such thing. A Master Carpenter knows how to make every part useful, every part beautiful.

And he is not done with his work in us yet.

Carpenter,
it helps so much to know you understand
what it's like to have an ordinary day.

*Sometimes it seems like I need to do
bigger and more impressive things. I
take comfort in the example of your life.
I pray that I will serve you faithfully
wherever you have me. Amen.*

THIRTY-THREE

Upholder

The LORD makes firm the steps
   of the one who delights in him;
though he may stumble, he will not fall,
   for the LORD upholds him with his
   hand.

Psalm 37:23–24

I lean my head against the shower wall and tears join the falling water. I am heart-weary, bone-aching. I have done my best to hold all this back. I told myself to get over it. I went for a walk. I brewed a pot of my favorite calming tea. But the dam has broken now, split wide, and there is nothing I can do to stop it.

"Jesus." I whisper his name because this is all I can muster in terms of a prayer. I will confess to you that it's flat-out hard to believe he is there. You have those moments too, don't you? The ones where faith feels like a mirage, like a story you've made up to make yourself feel better. But the reality is that no one is coming for you, no one really cares.

After I'm dry and dressed, I reach for my phone and leave a message for a friend. "I'm not okay," I say, "and I can't remember what's true. Will you please remind me?" She responds to the rescue flare I've shot into this night of my soul. She is swift and sure. She says that I am loved, not alone, stronger than I feel in this moment. God is with me and for me, she gently reminds.

I lean on her words, rest my tired self on them.

God knows our human selves can't feel what's spiritual sometimes, and so he comes for us in ways our frail earth-selves can understand. "The Word became flesh and made his dwelling among us" (John 1:14). And he becomes flesh again for us through our family, our friends, the kind stranger who lays a hand on our shoulder. Even through the wink of starlight and the song note of a red bird and the scent of morning coffee. Sometimes we need "Jesus with skin on," as Deidra Riggs likes to say.

Over the next few days, I see this again and again: An out-of-the-blue email from someone I hardly know saying they're praying for me. Encouragement from a podcaster who may never know she touched my life. An "I love you" and a kiss on my forehead from my husband. Even the beauty of a bare tree on a winter day with the first promise of spring showing green from its branches. All of these feel like the hand of God reaching out to steady me just when I feel as wobbly and unsure as the newborn calves in the farmer's field down the street.

When life begins to go downward or when I slip up, I fear I will never be able to recover. I will slide, slide, slide, and I will land in a place where there is no light or hope or coming back. But this is the promise we have: "Though she may stumble, she will not fall, for the Lord upholds her with his hand." I'm finding God's hand has many forms, many fingers, but it is ever-present if I reach for it, look for it, let it be the soft place where I land.

His nail-struck hands uphold us. His hands catch the tears streaming down in the shower. His hands set us on our feet over and over again. Yes, we will falter. *But we will not fall.* Not because we can hold it all together. But because we are always, mysteriously, held.

Upholder,
I'm so grateful for the security I have
in you. It's reassuring to know you will
hold me up. You will get me through
the hard times. You will be the One
who catches me, always. Amen.

THIRTY-FOUR

Great Reward

"Do not be afraid, Abram. I am your shield,
your very great reward."

Genesis 15:1

"What's in it for me?" It's the challenge posed by
sulky teenagers raising an eyebrow at a parent's
suggestion of a Disney family vacation. The wondering of a crossed-arms employee in another
meeting with spreadsheets and pie charts. The
asking of the good girl who serves and sweats
and tries so hard but secretly fights back tears and
resentment.

It is, whether we admit it or not, a common question of the human heart. We can trace its history back thousands of years.

One thing I love about the Bible is that the heroes are so very fallible, so uncensored and rough-edged, so unpolished and in progress. Like the moment when God came to Abram (later to be Abraham) and said, "I am your shield, your very great reward." The moviemakers would have the booming voice from the sky, Abram dropping to his knees in worship, the music rising in holy crescendo. But this Abram, the forefather of our faith, said instead, "Sovereign LORD, what can you give me?" (Gen. 15:2). Hadn't God just answered that question? Hadn't he just offered Abram his very self? Yet somehow it was missed, perhaps too grand or intangible to be comprehended. In other words, Abram asked, "But what's in it for me?"

At this point the producers might come up with a special effect, a bolt of lightning, or a whirling tornado. Abram's destruction for such insolence would be swift and Oscar worthy. But no, this God of ours seems to lean in and listen as Abram explains. He has no heir. He's confused. He's afraid. Then God took Abram outside and told him to look at the sky. God explained and reassured, promised and affirmed. And Abram believed him.

I think we need to know this story just like we need to know what we'd like the answer to be when we ask, "What's in it for me?" Pause for a moment and think about it. None of us are above this question. The response is most likely a longing of our hearts—love or acceptance or belonging.

Whatever it is, I believe God is still giving this answer: "I am your very great reward." He is acceptance. He is belonging. He is courage and hope and grace. Truth and strength and healing. Power and security and everything we long for most.

This is the irony: we, in return, often follow in Abram's footsteps and don't quite understand. "What can you give me?" we still ask too. And when the answer is unclear, we decide God must not have what we need after all. So we wear ourselves out searching for it. We people please or pad the bank account, work until we're weary, hunt for the perfect pair of jeans, try on lovers or lipstick. Teach

Sunday school. We are desperate beings with a hollowness inside us that demands to be filled.

God knows our tendency to ask, "What's in it for me?" and he doesn't shame or belittle us. He doesn't dismiss or destroy us. Jesus even asked, "What do you want me to do for you?" (Mark 10:51). It's not that God doesn't already know the answer; it's that he understands we are so often out of touch with what we really need most. We need to name it, to say it. He is tender with our doubt and fear, with our misdirected questions. He speaks to our hearts as he did with Abram. We only need to believe him.

Whatever we think we may want in this world, whatever we have told ourselves will make us whole, it is less than what's truly ours. What we really need to know is not "What's in it for me?" but "*Who* is in me?" The God who hung the stars in place, who hung on a cross on our behalf, is offering all of who he is to us. Our next question need not be if this will be enough but instead how we, tiny humans, will ever be able to contain everything he has to give us.

Great Reward,

it's an astounding mystery that you offer
me your very self. You did so on the cross,
and you do so each day. I have access
to all of who you are, to your unlimited
resources. What do I have to fear? Help me
bring all my hopes and longings to you, the
only One who can truly fill them. Amen.

THIRTY-FIVE

Advocate

I will ask the Father, and he will give you another advocate to help you and be with you
forever.

John 14:16

Sometimes a word flashes up from the pages of
my Bible like it's lit up from the inside, a holy neon
arrow or divine underlining. I'll look and see a
new truth in a story I've read 873 times. It's like
the tooth fairy placing a coin under my childhood
pillow after I checked and checked until my eyes
grew too heavy to stay open. I know now who put
the treasure there for me to find, and I know, too,

the One who makes Scripture "alive and active" (Heb. 4:12).

Sometimes this happens with the most ordinary of words, as it did this morning when I read in John 14:16: *another*. Normally I'd pass right over it. See it as insignificant and unessential to the point. But it lit up like Times Square, all glittery and flashy in my mind. Because it made me ask, "If the Spirit is *another* Advocate for us, then who are the others?"

It turns out we have all *three* members of the Trinity on our side in this way. Job said about God, "Even now my witness is in heaven; my advocate is on high" (Job 16:19). Then John tells us, "We have an advocate with the Father—Jesus Christ, the Righteous One" (1 John 2:1). And Jesus affirmed, "The Advocate, the Holy Spirit, whom the Father will send in my name, will teach you all things and will remind you of everything I have said to you" (John 14:26).

A few weeks ago my daughter, Lovelle, and I shared our story, how God brought us together when she was twenty after she'd spent time in the foster care system and other challenging situations. When we finished, my friend walked up to us and said, "My dad wants to meet you. He's a volunteer for CASA. He's staying with me right now, so I'll go pick him up from my house and bring him here." Lovelle and I nodded our heads. We knew CASA stood for "Court Appointed Special Advocates," an organization in our area that assigns representation to children who would otherwise have none. These advocates support and speak on behalf of kids in need, not as a group but personally, individually.

Soon my friend returned, her dad on her arm. He walked slowly with measured steps. "He had open heart surgery a week ago," she said, "but he really wanted to meet you." This kind and dignified man held a heart-shaped pillow against his chest, the same kind my grandpa had been given by the hospital to help the healing process after similar surgery. My friend's father stood there, leaning a bit, with strength in his voice and tears in his eyes as he explained his dreams for these kids. They were challenging, he said, but he wanted more for them. A better life. Hope. Wholeness. Peace. To break the cycle of brokenness. Oh, yes, they sometimes back talked him. They could be stubborn and didn't always listen. But he loved them. And, even more, he had chosen to always, always be there for them.

I knew then in a deeper way than ever before what this means: "God is for us" (Rom. 8:31). Jesus and the Holy Spirit are too. *All of divinity is an advocate for us in all our humanity.* This is a mystery and wonder to me. But I begin to grasp it when I close my eyes and think of my friend's father, hand over that huge heart pillow with scars underneath, telling us how these kids are worth standing up for no matter what they've done.

In the kingdom, we are those children. You. Me. Us. We are cherished and spoken up for and supported. Not because we are perfect or have earned it. Simply because of what our Advocates have already done for us, what they are doing even in this moment, and what they have promised to always, always do.

Advocate,

it is so powerful to know you are for me.
Jesus, thank you for dying and being
resurrected so that I could be forgiven.
Holy Spirit, thank you for guiding and
supporting me each day. God, thank you
for giving me right standing with you
through what your Son did on my behalf.
I understand I don't have to earn any of
this. I can only receive it—and I do. Amen.

THIRTY-SIX

One Who Sees

She gave this name to the LORD who spoke to her: "You are the God who sees me," for she said, "I have now seen the One who sees me."

Genesis 16:13

The early afternoon sun is just beginning to slant against the buildings as I step out of the car. I pull my jacket tighter around my shoulders. It's smooth leather, brown with a hint of gold and light in its tones. I am wearing it for a special occasion: a new photo being taken for the back cover of my next book.

Despite how it may sound, this is not a glamorous thing. There's no hairstylist or makeup artist standing by. No wardrobe assistant holding out a scarf. It's only me with my everyday makeup, an outfit I pulled from my messy closet this morning, and my hair barricaded against the breeze with nothing more than a bit of hairspray. I have asked a dear friend of mine who's gifted at finding the beauty around her to be the photographer. No fancy studio or lighting. And I have asked another friend—someone who loves me well, who has seen me barefaced with tears streaking my cheeks, and knows how my loudest laughter sounds—to come along for the photo shoot. I told my photographer friend, "I want to just have a conversation with the two of you and for you to capture my expressions as we go."

They join me and we find an old church, its brick bones resting in the shade. I say to my friends, "Tell me something funny." They giggle at this directness, which makes me do the same, and I hardly hear the click, click, click of the camera. When we finish about an hour later, I lean over the little screen of the camera and together we scroll back through. "Yes," I declare, "the one we need is there."

As I climb back into my car later, I realize having my picture taken this time wasn't hard or intimidating like it can tend to be. And I know in that moment what made the difference: *someone was looking at me through the eyes of love.* That changes everything. It's an uncomfortable thing to come under the gaze of a stranger. But there is something redemptive and grace-filled and soothing about having the eyes of someone who is so *for* us *on* us.

When we imagine how God might look at us, it can seem as if he must do so with the cool stare of a professional, as if he's analyzing us, finding the faults and flaws. But, no, he is looking at us as my camera-toting friend did. "The LORD watches over all who love him" (Ps. 145:20). Old Testament Hagar discovered this when she found herself alone in the desert with her child, sure they would soon die. God met her there, and while she felt as if she was seeing him for the first time, she realized he had seen her all along.

Wherever we are today, God sees not only our skin but also our souls, our strengths, and our scars. What we choose to show the world and everything we hide from it. And he loves every part of us. Not because we are perfect but because when he looks at us he also sees what Jesus did on the cross. Our sin has been washed away, the darkness has been defeated, and we have been restored to the beauty for which we were formed.

One day when we enter heaven, we will say with Hagar, "I have now seen the One who sees me." Until then, someone is always watching over us with love.

One Who sees,
you are the God who watches over me.
Thank you for looking at me through
eyes of love and seeing what's beautiful in
me even when I can only see brokenness.
Help me see myself more like you do. Not
because of what I've done but because
of what Jesus has done for me. Amen.

THIRTY-SEVEN

Freedom

> You will know the truth, and the truth will
> set you free.
>
> John 8:32

In childhood, freedom tastes like watermelon
seeds, sweet and smooth, spit onto the grass in
an impromptu contest between my cousins and
me. It smells of soda, sugary and warm, and the
tang of leftover chlorine from the pool. It feels
like the brush of grass against bare feet and the
stickiness of sweat down our necks and across our
shoulders. It sounds like the voices of our mamas
and daddies and grandparents. It looks like the
glow of fireworks, gold and red and blue, above

our heads or sparklers in our hands that we twirl like batons.

There is more to freedom too, things that can't be tasted or touched, seen or defined. This part of freedom isn't about what's present but rather what *isn't* there. When I think of those summer moments, there is no anxiety or striving, trying hard to be loved or believing lies about who I am. This deeper freedom is what I long for even more than apple pie and extra ice cream in my grown-up life.

I have looked for this freedom in many places, like a kid on a scavenger hunt. Perhaps it might be under the rock of recognition, high on the ladder of accomplishment, hiding in the corner of people pleasing, or waiting for me in that cardboard box of perfection. But what I truly longed for was never there. If you've experienced this too, then I have good news for both of us today.

What I'm finally discovering is that freedom is found in living in the truth. And truth is not a place. It's more than fact, opinion, or perception. For we who believe in Jesus, truth is a Person. Jesus said, "You will know the truth, and the truth will set you free," and "I am . . . the truth" (John 8:32; 14:6). How do we know true freedom in our lives? By knowing him.

This can sound mysterious, so let's talk about it the way we might as children—with all our senses. Knowing Jesus tastes like prayers, words on our lips from our hearts to his. It smells like bread or cream of mushroom casserole as we gather with other believers who share his love with us. It feels like the crinkle of paper beneath our fingers or a swipe across a screen as we intentionally read his Word each day. It sounds like saying, "I love you" or asking, "How can I help?" as we seek to serve like him in this world. It looks like having a connection with him that isn't just about intellect or education but also intimacy and experience.

Jesus frees our hearts from what holds us back—like our fear, perfectionism, and worry. We can be children again, loved and known, cared for and re, chasing fireflies and fireworks even with ll around us.

Freedom,

*you are the One who can release me from all
that binds me up inside. You are the Truth.
You are the Way. You are my Life. I want
to know you and love you always. Thank
you that I am your beloved child. Amen.*

THIRTY-EIGHT

Rescuer

He reached down from on high and took
    hold of me;
  he drew me out of deep waters. . . .
He brought me out into a spacious place;
  he rescued me because he delighted
    in me.

                        Psalm 18:16, 19

Niagara Falls roars and spills. She is magnificent in her power. She takes no prisoners. And yet, this morning, one has escaped her grasp. When we come to her edge, a crowd is lined up against a railing, hands over their mouths or wrapped protectively around the shoulders of those beside them.

It seems odd, this scene where carefree tourists
and smiles and the snapping of cameras should be.

"What's going on?" we ask a stranger. "Someone
went over the falls," he says, "and they are rescuing him." We lean over the edge and far below
us we see emergency workers with gear and cables,
bright jackets a contrast to the solemn gray rocks.
A man on a stretcher.

These rescuers have climbed down a steep wall.
They have put their lives in danger. Even now the
water rushes past relentlessly, without pity. It would
swallow them whole if it could. But it seems they
think about none of this as they work. They shout
and organize and then lift, lift, lift this man back to
safety. A helicopter comes, its blades whirring like
a giant benevolent bird. It flies away into blue and
we stand there stunned, unsure of what to do. The
man has injuries, but he will recover; he will live.
He is only the second person in history to do so
after going over the falls without the aid of a barrel
or any other buffer. We are witnesses to a miracle.

The rest of the day I keep picturing those rescue
workers. So diligent, so intent, so determined that

the outcome would be one of victory. They could have said, "This is too much to ask of us. He's on his own." They could have stood along the railing and just shook their heads.

But no, they changed the ending of the story.

And this is what our great God does too.

Because we are all the man going over the falls, whether from bravado or desperation or circumstances beyond our control. We sink and we wash up on shore, spent and broken. We are helpless and alone, in need and with nothing to offer. And into this, all of this, God shows up, saying, "I will send someone to rescue you." Jesus comes for us and does what we cannot. He stretches out on the cross. He breaks forth from the tomb. And we are lifted up from the place where we thought we'd never be able to escape from, where we thought it would all be over.

Even more outrageously, he does this not because it's his *job* but because he *loves* us. He does this when we first become his. But he does it again and again every time we fall or falter. He is the ever-present rescuer. The one who knows how prone we are to get ourselves into trouble, who understands we are human and weak. He knows the ways this world crashes over us and slams us against the rocks, and how we are in need of mending.

I still think of that man from time to time. I wonder what he did with his second chance at life. I think about what I will do with mine. Because this is the story of all of us. We are the rescued. We are the beloved. We are the living miracles.

Rescuer,

*thank you for coming for me even
when I didn't deserve it and never could
have earned it. You love me even in
my brokenness and you never leave me
where you find me. You lift me up and
you make me whole. You are worthy of
having all my days, all my praise. Amen.*

THIRTY-NINE

Potter

We are the clay, you are the potter;
we are all the work of your hand.

Isaiah 64:8

We walk through the door of a room that smells of earth and dirt, fallen trees, and ancient seasons. The table is rectangular, surrounded by a rainbow of small chairs. My daughter and I are decades ahead of our fellow participants in this clay class. The others are pig-tailed and freckled, dark-headed and clad in neon tennis shoes. "Did you know it would be like this?" she asks. "Nope," I reply. We grin.

I signed up for this class as part of my resolution to be a tourist in my hometown this year, to do things I never have before. I'd pictured fellow adults around me, a serious and substantial exercise. Instead, it's like art class in elementary school. Already the table is messy. Already it's clear I'm not among Picassos or Monets. I'm delighted and relieved.

We sit and the instructor points to a block of gray in front of us. "This is your clay. Today we are going to shape it into hearts." We trace outlines on the surface with a thin stick, then dig deep. All that is not necessary or useful is stripped away. We hold the hearts in our hands, and their cool, still surfaces grow warm and alive beneath our touch.

"Now you can design them however you'd like," the teacher says. My daughter chooses freehand. She swirls and writes. I use little presses to make polka dots and patterns. Hers will be spoon rests. Mine a set of ornaments. And I think of Jeremiah, sent by God to the potter's house, and how this prophet watched a craftsman with the clay, "shaping it as seemed best to him" (Jer. 18:4).

This work is intimate and personal. There is no mass production. No uniformity or conformity. It would be impossible to replicate one of these. Two little girls across from us gleefully push their hands into their pieces and I see fingerprints. If we ever wonder if God wants us to be like someone else, ever worry he's disinterested in the details of our lives, ever fret he's after machine-like perfection with us, then all we need to remember is that he is a Potter.

After we shape, we paint. But before this comes a disclaimer from the instructor: "When the clay goes through the fire, it will come out white." This is beautiful and familiar to me, the way trials bring out something unexpectedly lovely and strong in us. I choose red paint and follow lines and curves, working with care. And the whole time I have this vision in my mind of what will be. I work toward that, steadily, and when the form is imperfect, when it has dents or cracks, uneven edges or inconsistencies, I am not deterred. I understand this is the nature of clay.

And I come to understand, too, this clay has but one role: to yield itself to my care. It has nothing to worry about, to fear, to strive for as long as it remains in my hands. "Being confident of this, that he who began a good work in you will carry it on to completion until the day of Christ Jesus" (Phil.

1:6). We are dirt and we are the crafts of divinity. We are dust and delight. We are in progress and already perfectly loved.

At the end of the class, I look at the places where those plain gray slabs had been. Each one now holds a new creation. Some thick-skinned. Others delicate. Pink and yellow and blue. Some decorated with ponies and others looking suspiciously like pizza slices. None of them are museum- or art-gallery worthy. But they all have this in common: each reflects their maker in some way.

And I realize, suddenly, this was always the whole purpose, the entire point. To display the vision of the artist is what success looks like for clay.

Potter,

you are shaping me every day into who you want me to be. Thank you that the burden of becoming doesn't rest on me; you will complete the work you are doing in my life, in my heart. I yield every part of who I am to you. Amen.

FORTY

Husband

> For your Maker is your husband—
>   the LORD Almighty is his name—
> he Holy One of Israel is your Redeemer;
>   he is called the God of all the earth.
>
> Isaiah 54:5

I sit on a white ledge in our bathroom, bright pink hair dryer in one hand and stretchy black fabric in the other. My husband has biking class tonight and he accidentally left his shorts in the washer. I, nice wife that I am, volunteered to dry them the quickest way I know how. As I flip the spandex inside out, I see the padding all high-class biking shorts have to protect the rear of the rider (the source of many jokes in our household). From my angle, this particular padding looks suspiciously like a big red heart. I laugh out loud because, well, it's Valentine's Day, and this is not the kind of romance I'd pictured.

To my husband's credit, we'd celebrated early and he had my full blessing to go to his class tonight. Oh, it's taken a long time to get to this place of not demanding our life together be all about me. I've known the newlywed tears of realizing Saturday dates sometimes give way to vacuuming and laundry. I've gritted my teeth in frustration as I've learned lessons in communication. I've wanted to ask, on more than one occasion, "Why can't you just be more emotional like I am?" while at the same time knowing this is utterly ridiculous. Because even if that happened, if I woke up married to a clone of myself (help us all), I would still have the same issue: being married to a human.

I used to get mad at myself about this desire for a "perfect" partner. But I've come to realize that my desire is holy; it was simply my directing it toward my husband that needed altering.

There's a reason why we all long for the ultimate love story. Why so many of us put on sparkly tiaras even as little girls and look for the prince to come. Why we sigh wistfully at romantic comedies and weep silently at romantic tragedies. Why reality always seems to come up short when compared to fantasy. *A relationship with a man in this life was never supposed to be the fulfillment of the desire in our hearts.* It is only a preview and prototype of what we're created to experience with God in eternity.

Now I will tell you flat-out that this is a mystery to me. But over and over again God uses marital language to describe his relationship with his people. He is the bridegroom. We are the bride. He is the husband. We are the wife. He woos us. He cherishes us. He pursues our hearts. He stays faithful to us always. We are truly, deeply loved.

During an amicable conversation I once had with a young man from another religion, he asked, "Don't you think Christianity is presented as a love story as a way to market it to women? You know women like love stories!" I laughed at first, but then I said slowly and thoughtfully, "No, I think Jesus is *the* love story and all others are just imperfect copies. We're drawn to them because we're made for him." If we don't grasp this, then we will go searching for our "happily ever after" in places and people that can never hold it for us. We have one true love. We have one soul mate. We have only one better-than-a-fairy-tale prince.

We may get lovely glimpses of that in this life, but for now our vision is limited. We live out that grand love story in the day-to-day, with dirty dishes and spaghetti on the floor and shorts that get left in the washer too long. When we react by demanding that those around us fulfill all the needs within us, we set them up for failure. And when we expect everything to be perfect in the here and now, we set ourselves up for disillusionment.

We are the in-between people, the bride walking down the aisle, which on this earth sometimes seems more like a long dirt road. Still we press on in our white lace. We put a flower in our hair. We set our eyes on the horizon of this life. Because we are the hopers and the hopeless romantics, the ones who scandalously believe our forever-and-ever love story is only just beginning, and the best is yet to be.

Husband,

it seems strange to even use a name for you that has so much intimacy. But I know there is a longing inside me for perfect love, and you are the only one who can fulfill it. Help me look to you for what I need and want most. Thank you that I belong to you forever. Amen.

FORTY-ONE

Amen

These are the words of the Amen, the faithful
and true witness, the ruler of God's creation.

Revelation 3:14

It's a word familiar in my mouth. *Amen.* I said it
as a pig-tailed girl holding the hands of my family
around a dinner table where the smell of macaroni
and cheese made it hard to keep my eyes closed.
I've murmured it in church and even heard it
shouted on occasion, a proclamation. I've scrawled
it into the pages of my journal after pouring my
heart out to God in black ink. "A big *amen* to what
she said," I typed in an email as a way of agreeing
with encouragement offered to a hurting friend.

This word feels like a cousin to me. I've known it for so long. And yet so much of its meaning has been a mystery. I've thought it short and simple, straightforward and plain. But I'm coming to understand there's more to it than it seems, than what I have known when hearing it close a prayer before a hundred potlucks or after a thousand Sunday sermons. If you had asked me to define *amen*, I might have said, "The prayer is finished" or perhaps "I second that." But the real definition is much deeper and more beautiful. *Amen* means "So be it." It is a force word, a setting into action, a powerful alliance between us and heaven's will.

Amen is also a name of Jesus. He is *the* Amen (Rev. 3:14). So when we pray, when we say this word, we are actually calling on him. Second Corinthians 1:20 says, "For no matter how many promises God has made, they are 'Yes' in Christ. And so through him the 'Amen' is spoken by us to the glory of God." In other words, Jesus is God's "So be it."

When we ask God for a Savior, Jesus in the manger is the amen.

When we beg for forgiveness, Jesus on the cross is the amen.

When we need new life and hope, Jesus exiting the empty tomb is the amen.

When we long for comfort, peace, joy, and all that belongs to us as believers, Jesus in our everyday lives is the amen and amen and amen.

This doesn't mean we will automatically get what we want just by invoking this word. It is both a frustration and a relief to realize *amen* is not "So do it" but "So be it." Because this means, ultimately, when we say *amen*, we are praying for God's best and yielding to his will. Sometimes this is wonderful. Sometimes it is hard. Most often it's a bit of both.

What God does can be trusted because no matter what we ask for, his love for us through Jesus is the heart of the answer. This was true when my kid legs dangled off a kitchen chair and swung restlessly through a before-dinner blessing. It's true now when I bend my pajama-covered knees to the closet floor, a quiet place to pray. It will be true when my joints are as creaky as those beloved wooden pews and inside I'm skipping toward eternity.

This is what I know now, what I'll know forever: *amen* is more than where a prayer ends. It's where every answer begins—always and only with Jesus.

Amen,

you are the answer to everything I need.
You are the yes to every promise God has
made to us. You are my hope and the
One I can trust no matter what. Align
my heart with your will, who you are,
and who you want me to be. I love you.

FORTY-TWO

Healer

Praise the LORD, my soul,
    and forget not all his benefits—
who forgives all your sins
    and heals all your diseases,
who redeems your life from the pit
    and crowns you with love and
        compassion.

Psalm 103:2–4

I've sat by the wheelchair of a woman who told me how she, on the brink of slipping away, begged God to spare her life, to let her stay with her children. She was twenty-nine then. Her two little girls my mother and aunt. She lived to blow out birthday candles until there were close to eighty on her cake. She went home to heaven as we all wish to do, peacefully in her sleep. Prayer answered.

I've sat by the bedside of a man battling cancer, the pain lines creased across his forehead. Watching the in-out of his breath as I prayed when he couldn't. He was ninety-three. His time short. He was going to her, to the wife who'd made it home first. Healing looked different than it had before. He joined her and Jesus at midnight on Father's Day. Prayer answered.

Earlier this week, a friend's husband dropped suddenly at dinner. At the time I'm writing this, he's suspended between this life and the next. An online group has formed to share words of comfort, verses, tears, and songs. And in it all, there is this underlying wild belief that whether he wakes up here or in the presence of Jesus, the outcome will be the same: prayer answered.

To call God Healer is a brave, unnatural thing, because he is mysterious in his ways, unpredictable in his plans, and sometimes beyond comprehension in his methods of medicine. It takes trust and gritted teeth and the salt of tears on our cheeks.

It's tempting to say, "You are good only if you heal in the way and time we want." But what we are asked to do is instead whisper or shout or groan, "You are good *even if not*."

This surrender grieves and distresses and stretches us. And I believe God gets this; he mourns with us. Jesus wept outside the tomb of Lazarus even though he knew his friend would be resurrected in just a few moments. This world and those in it are broken in ways God never intended, and he is determined there will be a day all is made right, when he forever wipes away not only our tears but his too.

And his compassion applies not only to our bodies, so frail, but also to our hearts. The sin-sickness, rejection infection, ravages of addiction, scratch marks of fear, limp of loss, fracture of relationships—humanity is a walking hospital filled with the wounded. God is in the halls, in every room, caring about and tending to every bit of it. From the faintest sneeze to the shattered soul. Our pain is never too small or too big for him. His relentless desire is to bring us into complete wholeness and health. He proved it by stretching out on a cross, by taking our pain and making it his. It is "by his wounds we are healed" (Isa. 53:5).

The verb in that verse is present tense—"we *are* healed." It has already happened. It is already true. This means when we pray for healing there is never an "if," only a "when" and a "how." Some in eternity, some now. What God does is about his eternal purposes and faithfulness, not our efforts or the size of our faith We don't have to try hard or be good to get the answer we want. God is not a manipulator; he is a comforter and miracle-maker.

So we wait. We pray. We wrestle. We hope. Sometimes we rejoice. Sometimes we weep. And always we give ourselves over to the only Healer, with healed, nail-scarred hands.

Healer,

this broken world is hard to live in
sometimes. You understand that because
you have been here too. You've known

pain, and you have compassion for us.
Please bring healing in the ways you
know are best even when it's beyond my
understanding. I trust you with my heart,
body, life, and those I love. Amen.

FORTY-THREE

Faithful

Let us hold unswervingly to the hope we pro-
fess, for he who promised is faithful.

Hebrews 10:23

A handsome young produce peddler in a 1932
Ford Roadster, a group of pretty girls walking
with books in their arms. The car slows, the door
opens, a friendly greeting, giggles. They climb in
for a ride to high school, but the driver and one
passenger have just begun a much longer journey
together. John and Ann will elope soon after; she
only seventeen, with a father planning to marry
her to a much older man. Their elopement seems

an act of passion, even desperation. The cynics surely said, "It will never last."

The cynics were wrong.

John and Ann married over eighty-four years ago and are now both over one hundred years old. They have fourteen grandchildren, sixteen great-grandchildren, and the honor of being America's "longest-married couple."[1] As you might imagine, folks want to know their secrets. So one Valentine's Day a company hosted John and Ann on Twitter—something the couple never could have imagined in 1932—and let the online crowd ask questions. John's and Ann's answers seemed unglamorous in many ways. No mention of scarlet roses or private jets, serenades or grand gestures. John says, "We struggled in the beginning, but, luckily, we were content with what we had. It's just important to be content with what you have."[2] Ann offers, "You won't get any romance out of him. It's a devotion. Why do you have to explain it . . . ?"[3]

Ann asks a valid question: Why do you have to explain it when you've lived it so long it's like breathing? As I look through their answers again,

I find a theme between the lines. The real secret to their togetherness, their decade-after-decade commitment is this: faithfulness. It's the less sexy, unshiny, overlooked part of every great relationship. Yet it's just as essential as its more celebrated and recognized counterpart, love.

In Scripture, the two appear side by side again and again:

> Love and faithfulness meet together; righteousness and peace kiss each other. (Ps. 85:10)

> Let love and faithfulness never leave you; bind them around your neck, write them on the tablet of your heart. (Prov. 3:3)

> Through love and faithfulness sin is atoned for. (Prov. 16:6)

"Love and faithfulness" are used together more than ten times to describe who God is as well.

Faithfulness is a term we instinctively understand but, like Ann, struggle to explain. After looking at several definitions and pondering for a bit, here is my official version, courtesy of my Southern roots. Faithfulness is what folks around here like to call *stick-to-itiveness*. It means you see it through, stay committed, hold on in the ups and downs. It's the "for better or worse" in the vows. It's a relentless resilience that simply will not give up, give in, or let go—no matter what.

This is how God loves us. His commitment to us doesn't waver based on how "good" we are on any given day. It doesn't depend on our performance or perfection. Our divine partner isn't waiting to walk out and slam the door behind him because we forgot the milk or burned the toast or hogged the sheets. Or much, much worse.

And God asks that we, in return, be faithful to him too. That we don't shred our commitment when the prayer isn't answered or the plans don't work out or we just can't feel his love for us even though it's as real as the sun above us.

John and Ann have shared over eighty-four years on this earth. We're likely to share just as long with our God—followed by forever. As Ann says, "It's a lifelong thing. How do you define love?

Through actions, understanding, little things."[4] In other words, through faithfulness. One moment, one day, one eternity at a time.

Faithful God,

*you are the only One who will be with
me every day of my life here on this earth
and forever in heaven. You are my love,
my partner, my soul's best friend, and so
much more. Help me stay fully devoted to
you. And thank you that you promise you
will be fully faithful to me too. Amen.*

FORTY-FOUR

Giver

> He who did not spare his own Son, but gave
> him up for us all—how will he not also, along
> with him, graciously give us all things?
>
> Romans 8:32

We sit on two stools and a chair with red pillows piled high in front of my fireplace. We adjust the camera angle on my phone—up, then down. We tuck stray hair behind our ears one last time, make jokes, and try to stop laughing before the screen counts down three, two, one. Then we are live on the internet. Suzie Eller, Jennifer Watson, and I are doing the latest episode of what we've dubbed "More than Small Talk." We have conversations about struggles and fears, the real and the everyday, what we know to be true and what we're still learning so very slowly.

Today we're talking about comparison, and we all own up to battling it—that sneaky old beast that would like to take bites out of our joy, contentment, and identity. Suzie has asked a group of women how it shows up in their lives, with its scaly tail and snapping jaws. One woman describes comparison in a way we all might. She says, "Sometimes it feels like someone else is living my dream." "Oh," we say in unison when this phrase is uttered; yes, sometimes it seems that way.

I felt tempted to believe this lie of comparison during our years of infertility. And I've watched its shadow cross faces in high-stakes corporate meetings, at conferences full of hopeful writers, at the local pool, in the makeup aisle of the grocery store, all the places where there are humans. We can come to believe, somehow, that God must be holding out on us. This temptation goes all the way back to the Garden of Eden, where Eve listened to the serpent, who implied God was denying her something she should have. Something she deserved. Something she was entitled to. The enemy of our hearts would still have us believe the same about our relationship with God.

Because if we see God as stingy, the old miser doling out a single bread crumb when he has a cupboard full of cookies, then we will always feel resentful or cheated. We will believe someone else is getting just a little bit more. We will not be able to trust or rest or joyfully receive. But God is not Scrooge, not a save-it-all-for-a-rainy-day withholder, not a hoarder, killjoy, or selfish grasper. He is an extravagant Giver.

> No good thing does he withhold from those whose walk is blameless. (Ps. 84:11)

> He who did not spare his own Son, but gave him up for us all—how will he not also, along with him, graciously give us all things? (Rom. 8:32)

> Every good and perfect gift is from above, coming down from the Father of the heavenly

lights, who does not change like shifting shadows. (James 1:17)

We can get confused about that last bit, the part that talks about what's "good and perfect." We look at what someone else has and say, "That would be so good for me. It would be truly perfect." But just because something is good for someone else doesn't mean it's God's best for us, even though it seems so lovely and shiny.

During almost a decade of infertility, I looked at a thousand round-cheeked babies and thought, *Yes, that would be good.* Instead, God sent me a twenty-year-old daughter and declared, "This is best." I never would have guessed. But he was so right. Sometimes God's provision doesn't look like what we planned. Sometimes it's hard to understand. Sometimes we don't even fully see it until eternity. But we can trust it will always be generous and kind and wise.

My conversation with Suzie and Jennifer draws to a close and we click finish on the little screen. The camera stops. But of course we're not really done. We have so much more to discover about our humanness and the God who made us. The One who also created every blessing we've ever known—the fiery blue of a dragonfly's wing, the taste of watermelon on a summer day, the kiss of someone we love on our forehead, the cross, the resurrection, the forever home waiting.

God is not holding out *on* us.

He is holding out his hands *to* us.

They are filled with all we need. And more than we've yet imagined.

Giver,

everything good in my life comes from you. All I have and all I am are because of you. Thank you that you never withhold what's best from me. Instead, you love and provide extravagantly. I want to share what you've so freely given. Amen.

same

Jesus Christ is the same yesterday and today
and forever.

Hebrews 13:8

I am nine, sitting cross-legged on an elementary-
school gym floor that smells vaguely like rubber
soles and ketchup. My friends and I are lined up in a
row, waiting to go to recess or art class or the library.
We're likely wearing neon shorts and scrunchies
in our side ponytails; children of the eighties. The
girls nearest me lean in, grinning, and say, "We want
to tell you something. We're best friends." I look
back and forth between the two of them, confused,
because just yesterday the one with the strawberry
hair told me that *I* would always be her best friend.

I ride my bike home alone that day, forlorn, and sit at the kitchen table with a cookie in my hand and my mama across from me. These things happen, she explains gently. I nod, feeling very grown-up and wise, even in my disappointment. I will think of this again when my crush flirts with me one day and holds the hand of a long-legged athlete the next. I will feel it when the conversation with the editor at the conference seems to go so well and then the rejection letter comes in the mail. I will revisit it when the whirling crowd online is landing on my site today and taking off to another one the next like a flock of spring sparrows.

It is the nature of humans to be fickle. We put rings on each other's fingers and then signatures on divorce papers. We are employee of the month and then find ourselves on the layoff list. We are dear friends and then time and space and life make us drift until we're looking back at old photos and thinking, *I haven't seen her in a while*. Yet we keep searching, hoping, longing for that person who will stay. The constant who will never go away.

In these moments, it comforts me to know "Jesus Christ is the same yesterday and today and forever" (Heb. 13:8). He isn't going to pick someone else on the playground. He isn't going to bring us roses and then forget to call the next day. He won't recruit us for the pet project and then neglect to invite us to the celebration party. He won't use us up and throw us out, pull us close and then push us away, whisper in our ear and then lose our phone number. Because his love for us isn't based on our charm; it's rooted in his character. It doesn't come from his emotions but instead from an eternal commitment. It isn't dependent on what we do for him, but what he's already done for us.

It gets even better: Jesus also tells us, "I am making everything new!" (Rev. 21:5). Who he is doesn't change, yet he moves and pursues in endlessly creative ways. It's what our hearts long for, what we're really looking for when we exchange the friendship bracelets or say the vows or sit down at the desk in a new office for the first time. We want to know we can trust, completely, the one with whom we have aligned ourselves. And yet we also want to know that doing so will lead to life and growth and adventure. We want stability and excitement, consistency and change, familiarity and novelty.

When we try to demand all of this from a human being, we always end up disappointed. But the answer isn't to shut down our hearts, to tell ourselves we're being unrealistic or irrational. Instead, it's to take those desires to the One who put them there in the first place, the only One who can truly fulfill them. Jesus "is the same yesterday and today and forever" (Heb. 13:8), yet he also says, "I am making everything new!" (Rev. 21:5). Both are what we need. Both are eternally true.

One Who
Stays the Same,
it's so comforting to know that who you
are and your love for me will always be
faithfully steady. And yet you invite me to
a life filled with new adventures too. I trust
you, and I will follow you. Only you can
fulfill all the desires of my heart. Amen.

FORTY-SIX

Caretaker

Cast all your anxiety on him because he cares
for you.

1 Peter 5:7

I stand in a sea of people. A wave of business travelers with their dark suits and polished leather bags walks by, deep in conversation about spreadsheets and mergers. A family follows, two toddlers pointing out the ice-cream vendor to a sleep-deprived mama with a weary hand up to her forehead. A high school sports team comes next, loud and high-fiving in jerseys the color of four-leaf clovers.

"Are you ready?" my husband asks. "We need to get to the gate." I nod, but the reality is, I'm tired.

Long flights. Big airports. Heavy bags. I lag behind Mark as he strides in front of me. At some point he turns around and looks at my computer bag, the one slung across my shoulder that's making my back ache and slowing me down. He reaches out his hand. "I'll take that for you," he says, and I watch as my manly man proceeds down the corridor with a girly bag in hand. Because he loves me. I stand a little taller, pick up the pace, bypass the tempting scent of coffee. We arrive just as our boarding announcement comes over the speakers.

I think of this moment months later when I read these words: "Cast all your anxiety on him because he cares for you" (1 Pet. 5:7). *What does that really mean?* I wonder. I find the answer: "the word 'casting' used in 1 Peter 5:7 was the Greek word *epiripto*, a compound of the words *epi* and *ripto*. The word *epi* means *upon*, as *on top of something*. The word *ripto* means *to hurl, to throw,* or *to cast,* and it often means *to violently throw* or *to fling something with great force.*"[1]

That day in the airport, I couldn't get rid of my heavy bag fast enough. I didn't second-guess my husband's offer. I didn't try to press on out of pride. I let go of that weight as quickly as I could. But the same isn't always true in my everyday life. Instead of casting my cares, I caress them. I pull them close and guard them. And all the while Jesus is saying, "Here, let me take that for you." Thankfully, Jesus understands this is the way of humans. We can be slow to surrender. We have a tendency to cling to what weighs us down. So he offers not once but again and again, gently and with great compassion. It's never too late to take him up on his compassion.

The word *anxiety* in 1 Peter 5:7 also means more than I originally thought. It's not just that fluttery feeling in our chests, not only the worry that barks at us in the night. It describes any trouble or difficulty, any challenge or hardship, all the fears and uncertainties. Every bit of it.

I write these words about releasing our cares, knowing this is more easily said than done. I have a nervous system that leans toward stress. My fear circuits are sensitive. Sometimes it seems I battle worry all the time, every day. Do I always immediately hand over the bag? No. Often I carry it until I simply can't anymore, until it slips from my shoulders because I'm flat-out exhausted and can't take another step. But you know what? Jesus takes it even then. And I am learning, slowly, to let go sooner.

Knowing Jesus is my caretaker isn't an easy fix. It's not a simple one-time solution. For me, this truth means there is always hope. It means I'm discovering a different, freer way of being. It means I'm believing that by the time I reach my final destination, I will be traveling so much lighter.

Caretaker,

thank you for so graciously taking my burdens, fears, and anxieties. Nothing is too big for you to carry and nothing is too small for you to care about. I choose to release what's been weighing me down into your loving hands. Amen.

FORTY-SEVEN

Rest

Truly my soul finds rest in God;
 my salvation comes from him.

Psalm 62:1

We have a couch like a mama bear. She's protective, this piece of furniture, and when you curl into her, she'll wrap around you with her big arms and let you rest on her lap. She's old and tattered and soft in all the right places. Last Saturday she seemed to whisper, "Come here, little one." I obeyed and slept in her embrace like no one could ever harm me, like all the world could fall to pieces outside the window and I would be untouched. Hours later I woke and gasped when I saw the clock. *I was so tired*, I thought, *and I didn't even know it.*

Surely I'm not the only one. When *USA Today* did a multiyear poll, they found people to be busier with every turn of the calendar, women especially.[1] Yet I am coming to a place in life where I am beginning to understand that busy may be enticing, but it's not always best.

I first began to consider this when I stood on the brink of burnout almost two years ago. I had trouble making myself get out of bed and go through the day. Conversations hurt. Tasks felt like boulders. I fantasized about running away to become a barista in Australia. *Then Jesus.* He told me I didn't have anything to prove. He whispered that I was loved as I am. He taught me that what I needed was not to perform but to be a person. And, perhaps most of all, he began to help me understand what it is to live in rest.

Oh, I am still learning. My mama bear couch can testify to that fact. But I have at least come this far: I now know that rest is not laziness, not a lack of responsibility or willingness to do our part. It is a gift from a loving God's heart.

We see this thread all through Scripture. In Genesis, just after creation, God rested as a model for us. He brought his people out of the striving of Egypt to the promised land of Canaan, which literally means "the resting place."² He is the Shepherd in Psalms who makes us lie down in green pastures, leads us beside still waters, and restores our souls. In the Gospels, Jesus offers this: "Come to me, all you who are weary and burdened, and I will give you rest" (Matt. 11:28). And at the end of time, "there remains, then, a Sabbath-rest for the people of God" (Heb. 4:9). Rest, not hustle, has always been and will always be God's desire and design for us.

In our culture, we define rest narrowly. We see it as simply stopping our work. But to God it is so much more. Rest is a state of peace and security. Yes, sometimes it is an actual, tangible pause, but it is also a way of living differently no matter what we're doing. I have stared at the ceiling in the night, completely still, and not been tranquil at all as worries shook my mind. I have been in the middle of giving a speech to thousands and felt absolutely at peace inside even though my lips and schedule and words seemed to be moving at warp speed.

Yes, our bodies need regular rest, but I think that is only the first layer, the very surface of what God wants for us. Isaiah says, "Those who hope in the LORD will renew their strength. They will soar on wings like eagles; they will run and not grow weary, they will walk and not be faint" (40:31). In other words, rest is not simply the lack of activity but the presence of trust. Because trust is a kind of inner leaning, an intentional reliance on someone else. This means, as David writes in the psalms, God himself is our true rest.

I am finding him to be more like the mama bear couch with the big arms than I first thought, except it's our hearts he holds. The world falls to pieces, the toddlers holler, the phone call brings an earthquake, the neatly written to-do list becomes a rowdy volcano, but we don't have to be over-whelmed or overcome. We can live in rest because we live in God's love always, from our quietest moments to our busiest days.

Rest,

help me pause in this moment and lean into where I belong, a place of peace and security in you. Thank you that I can come to you, rely on you, and you will hold me through whatever today brings. Amen.

FORTY-EIGHT

Forgiver

In him we have redemption through his blood,
the forgiveness of sins, in accordance with the
riches of God's grace.

Ephesians 1:7

Crumpled tissues create a fortress in front of me,
flanked by medicine bottles. I'm behind them,
slumped down, surrendering to sleep at last. My
husband comes into the room and says something.
I struggle to hear, to process through the fog. But I
miss what he's trying to express entirely. Instead, I
misunderstand. I snap. Angry words. Then tears.
A retreat to our bedroom. A slammed door. I'm a

crazy woman, out of my mind. What am I doing? What am I saying?

I don't trust myself to calm down or behave. So, still in my pajamas, I grab my purse and walk out the door. I back up the car and then sit in the street, unsure of where to go, what to do. I'd likely give our entire town the plague if I entered a public space, and besides, I don't feel well enough to take another step.

Then a moment of pure Southern inspiration: my vehicle begins the familiar journey to the Chick-fil-A drive-through. I get my waffle fries and a diet Dr Pepper, effective as any prescription. I pull into the final row of the parking lot.

I call my friend and say something like, "I had an epic meltdown and I can't calm myself down and I'm in the parking lot in my pajamas eating fries." She tries to understand me between bites and might have stifled a giggle before she tells me this is not the end of the world and, no, I am not the worst human ever.

She convinces me to go home. "Sleep," she says. "Sleep and then work it out." I walk back through the door of my house, repentant and exhausted. I crawl under the covers and wake three hours later. I go to our living room, to the mama-bear red couch. I sit on it and wait, unsure of how to proceed. My husband comes out from his office and eyes me warily, as one might a normally docile pet who has recently taken up biting. I pat the couch to let him know it's safe. He sits beside me and the tears come—a river, a flood. "I'm sorry," I say. "I'm so sorry."

Surely he's going to reprimand me. He's going to tell me all I've done wrong not just today but in all our marriage. He's going to make me feel the shame I deserve. I am ready. I have it coming. But instead, my husband looks at me, puts his arm around my shoulders, and says only, "None of us are at our best all the time." This is it. All he offers. The end. I lean into his shoulder and I almost can't receive it.

But then somehow I do, and I feel loved, so loved, in a deeper way than I even do in my best moments. Because in those I-have-it-all-together times, it can seem as if somehow I have earned the affection and the accolades and the acceptance. But I know, with my messed-up hair and messed-up words and cough-syrup stains, that I've got nothing to offer just then. Not a thing.

I think of Jesus and how he knows what's true about us too—that we are not always at our best. We act as if he will be shocked and surprised and dismayed when we fail or falter. But hasn't he known what we are capable of all along? Isn't that why he came? And when we come to him in that state, broken and sick, sorry and hurting, he doesn't offer condemnation. He offers compassion. "It is finished," he said on the cross. It is over. It is done. You are forgiven.

Some folks would say this is getting off too easy, that we will all go wild if we fully believe this to be true. But I know the next few days after my husband spoke this way to me that I wanted, more than ever, to please him and to bless him and to bring him joy. Because this is the response love evokes in us. When we are granted grace, we live from that place.

I hope I never end up eating waffle fries quite like that again (they taste better with ketchup than shame). And I hope you never follow my greasy-fingered example. But we are human, you see, and if we find ourselves in such a situation, at least now we know more about what to do. We'll know we can go, right away, still in our pajamas and holding our tissues, to the God who loves us. The One who has seen us at our worst and still, always, loves us best.

Forgiver,
through your death on the cross and
resurrection I'm forgiven, accepted as I am
and able to grow into all you've created me
to be. Thank you for covering my sin and
mistakes with your grace and love. Amen.

FORTY-NINE

Perfecter

By one sacrifice he has made perfect forever
those who are being made holy.

Hebrews 10:14

I type the word *perfect* into the little box on one
of my favorite sites and the parade begins. Perfect eyebrows. Perfect Christmas photos. Perfect
strawberry cheesecake. Perfect messy bun (which
seems to me like a contradiction). I feel my heart
beating anxiously as I look and read. Am I dizzy?
Is it hot in here? *Perfect* and I have a complicated
relationship.

On this day I'm ready to start figuring it out,
and I begin with this phrase: "Jesus . . . perfecter

of faith" (Heb. 12:2). I go poking around in thick books to find an answer—Hebrew and Greek dictionaries, commentaries written by folks who have fancy letters after their names. This is what I find: in our modern world and language, *perfect* means "flawless." But in biblical terms, it is different. It is something more like "whole" and "complete." When we say *perfect*, we think supermodel with twig-like limbs. When Scripture says *perfect*, it's more like a tree growing, roots going deeper, branches spreading wider, fruit ripening in the afternoon sun.

The commercials and the touched-up magazines, the carefully arranged photos and the highly edited pitches would have us believe that perfect is a product. You can buy it or build it, force it or find it. But instead, perfect is a mysterious, sacred process.

Hebrews tells us, "By one sacrifice he has made perfect forever those who are being made holy" (10:14). When Jesus died on the cross, he said, "It is finished." So when we receive what he did on our behalf, we are instantly and eternally *positionally* perfect in God's eyes. It is done. We are the broken made whole. Yet we live on this earth and we are still learning to live out who we already are; we are being made more like Jesus every day.

I think this is the context we need to remember when we read, "Be perfect, therefore, as your heavenly Father is perfect" (Matt. 5:48). I've heard Bible-thumping preachers holler this from a pulpit as a way to coerce folks into acting a bit more proper. But to think we can be as perfect as God is not only ignorant but also incredibly arrogant. And just after this, Jesus said, "Be careful not to practice your righteousness in front of others" (Matt. 6:1). He seems to understand the first response of the human heart to hearing, "Be perfect" is to say, "I have to try really hard and be very good." At this point his audience surely wondered, *Well, then, how is it possible for me to be perfect?* Jesus himself is the answer to this question.

We don't need a list of rules to keep. We need a Savior. We don't need to get our acts together. We need a loving God who acts on our behalf.

We don't need to be without flaws. We need to understand that perfect is always and only about faith. It's not something we do; it's something we believe and receive through Jesus's death on the cross and resurrection.

What does that look like in our practical lives? It means even when we don't want to crinkle those "perfect" eyebrows, we choose to say to a friend, "I'm not okay. Will you pray for me?" It means when the family photos turn into an eye-rolling, ugly-crying mess, we hug each other and try again. It means when the strawberry cheesecake has a crack like the Grand Canyon down the middle, we serve it anyway because it's about blessing not impressing. It means our messy-bun selves sometimes go to the grocery store in yesterday's yoga pants and don't hide when we see someone we know.

We don't have to hide from Jesus either, even in our most human moments. Because this is our story and our truth and our sure hope: we are imperfect women who are perfectly loved by a perfect God.

Perfecter,

you have made me perfect and you are
growing me into all you created me to be.
I pray you will help me trust you in the
process and stop trying to make myself
perfect. Thank you for what you have done
and are still doing in and for me. Amen.

FIFTY

Purpose-Giver

But the plans of the LORD stand firm
forever,
  the purposes of his heart through all
  generations.

Psalm 33:11

I stand at the sink, dirty pan in hand. I smell citrus in the soap, hear the warm water flow, move the brush in circles over the last bits of burnt cheese. I feel small in this space, ordinary and rooted to the ground. I have been here for a long while now, in this kitchen, on this earth, and I silently ask, *What's my purpose?*

Across the street a mama or grandma might be asking the same as she changes the tenth baby diaper of the day. Maybe in the center of town someone is leaning her head on her desk with the door closed, just resting for a moment on that stack of spreadsheets and wondering this too.

When we ask this question and silence seems to be the answer, we often go searching. We'll say yes to another opportunity or perhaps run away from it all. We'll join that cool play group or volunteer at the soup kitchen on Fridays. We might jockey for the promotion or put in the long hours. *My purpose is out there somewhere*, we think, *and one day I'll find it.*

But then the opportunity doesn't go as planned or the giving leaves us empty, and our souls grow pale in the fluorescent light. "Something else will do it," we say. "Surely it will be the next thing." And on we go with our gypsy hearts.

It's understandable, this great migration. We live in a culture that tells us the purpose of life is about *us*. We must find that *one thing* we are here to do and then all will be well; we will be whole. But when I look closer at how *purpose* is used in Scripture, there's a different story.

> The plans of the Lord stand firm forever, *the purposes of his heart* through all generations. (Ps. 33:11, emphasis added)

> Many are the plans in a person's heart, but it is *the Lord's purpose* that prevails. (Prov. 19:21, emphasis added)

> And we know that in all things God works for the good of those who love him, who have been called according to *his purpose*. (Rom. 8:28, emphasis added)

The purposes of his heart, the Lord's purpose, his purpose—over and over when purpose is described, it comes from God and belongs to him. Also, purpose isn't talked about much in terms of just individual people. It is more often spoken of as an ongoing thread that stretches through all of history and eternity. It is so much bigger than we are. So when we go looking only for "our" purpose, we are disappointed. What changes everything is when we understand that a meaningful life is not just about finding our purpose but joining God's.

In other words, we inquire, "What matters most to you, God?" Someone asked Jesus this and here is his answer: "Jesus replied: 'Love the Lord your God with all your heart and with all your soul and with all your mind.' This is the first and greatest commandment. And the second is like it: 'Love your neighbor as yourself'" (Matt. 22:37–39).

If we want to be part of God's purposes today, then we simply love him, others, and ourselves. That means standing at the kitchen sink washing dishes can be worship. It means that another diaper changed can be an act of sacred service. It means the work project done well can be an offering. It means we don't have to find purpose only "out there." It can also be "right here."

The square of earth you are standing on is the only place in all of history and the entire universe where both you and God are right now. It's where his purposes and you, a person created by him, come together. This is not small or inconsequential. It is beautiful and powerful. It is holy, meaningful ground.

Purpose-Giver,
you are the One who is working out his
purposes in all of history, eternity, and
me. Show me how to use who and where
I am in ways that bring you joy. You give
every moment of my life meaning. Amen.

FIFTY-ONE

Word

The Word became flesh and made his dwelling among us. We have seen his glory, the glory of the one and only Son, who came from the Father, full of grace and truth.

John 1:14

I take a seat in front of a microphone that stretches toward me as if it's a curious, long-necked goose. I'm tempted to pat it and tell it that I mean no harm, to offer it a bit of the granola bar stuffed in my purse so that it will be kind to me in the next few moments.

I'm here to record a few one-minute messages of encouragement for our local Christian radio station. The capable producer sitting across from me is also a dear friend, and before official business begins, we chat for a few moments. I tell her of my busy schedule and the racing thoughts that have been waking me up at night. "I'm going to figure out how to honor my personal capacity," I tell her. "I'm not going back to living this way." She nods in solidarity and with understanding. She shares some struggles that have been weighing on her as well.

Then it's time to hit record, and I begin to read from the paper in front of me.

> Our worry can't change the world, only God can. Luke 12:25 says, "Who of you by worrying can add a single hour to your life?" Jesus, in all His gentleness and kindness, His extravagant mercy and care, wants to take the burdens from our hands and say, "You don't have to carry this anymore."[1]

When I finish, my friend and I look at each other and grin. Because I have just shared what both of us needed to hear. I pulled this paragraph from a blog post I wrote months ago. Yet in this moment, in this space, it feels new and alive.

When we think of Jesus being the "Word," we can picture dusty old Bibles with red letters and thick ribbon bookmarks, the kind that are set on coffee tables or shelves. But the Word is "alive and active" because the Word is a Person (Heb. 4:12). This has always been so.

"In the beginning was the Word, and the Word was with God, and the Word was God. He was with God in the beginning. Through him all things were made; without him nothing was made that has been made" (John 1:1–3). The Word created peacocks and tomatoes and the freckle on your nose. Then the Word came into that creation. He took on flesh—he had eyelashes and elbows and pinky toes. He walked dirty streets and ate fish roasted over open fires and napped on the deck of a boat. In other words, *the Word has always been about the spiritual becoming the tangible, the divine entering our everyday lives.*

So in that moment when I spoke Scripture out loud along with the truth God revealed to my heart through it, something came into being that hadn't been before--new peace and hope in our hearts. And Jesus came into that little recording studio in a powerful way even though, yes, he'd been there all along. The Word speaks to us where we are—in the quiet moments of the morning, in conversations with friends who love him too, in churches and boardrooms and bedrooms, in recliners and recording studios.

The Word is more than lines on a page. He is the narrator of our lives. He is the beginning and the end and the middle of the story. He is still creating, still coming into the ordinary moments, still speaking to every heart willing to listen.

Word,
you are the One who knows my heart
best, and you are the source of the truth
I need in every circumstance. Your voice
is always full of love. What do you want
to say to me today? I will listen. Amen.

FIFTY-TWO

Name above All Names

God exalted him to the highest place and gave him the name that is above every name, that at the name of Jesus every knee should bow, in heaven and on earth and under the earth, and every tongue acknowledge that Jesus Christ is Lord, to the glory of God the Father.

Philippians 2:9–11

Honor roll. Sports rankings. Election outcomes. Get your name to the top of the list, this world says. Our hearts have their own lists too. Be the most popular. The best mom. The hardest worker. If you asked me, I would say, "Oh, none of that matters to me." But my life has sometimes told a different story. I know what it is to hustle, to try to prove my worth, to show everyone I am good enough. Perhaps I'm not the only one.

We have an inner drive for meaning, for affirmation, and for validation. We want to know we matter. We count. We are doing it right. What better way than to push our name to the top? Yes, spell it out in black and white so I can see my worth. Then everyone else will believe it too.

In all our well-intentioned striving, we can miss one thing: the top spot on every list is already taken. Jesus has "the name that is above every name."

I picture his name in red, scrawled in a high school yearbook above the most-liked list. This name says to the awkward girl on the last row of the class picture, the one who only has a quarter of her face visible because she's learned to hide, "I see you. I know you. I value what you have to offer."

This name is above the hall of fame showcases, the walls lined with accomplishments, and the photos of human wonders. If we listen closely, it whispers, "You are not what you do. You are not defined by your greatest moments—or your worst."

That name is found on the invisible list the sweat pants–wearing woman who shows up late for school pick-up is making in her mind. She watches the other moms. *She's prettier than I am. She's more organized. She's better at small talk.* And the Name says, "There is no comparison in the kingdom. You are not more or less than anyone else. You are mine and that's what matters."

We don't have to make a name for ourselves because we belong to the One with the highest, best name. We've looked at more of what that means together on these pages. We've seen who God is: Creator, Friend, Giver, and so much more. We've also explored who we are in him: loved, chosen, cherished. When we know this, we begin to live from a different perspective. We understand we are small and yet hugely significant. We see we have an important place in God's story, but we are not the author. We realize hard times will come, but there is One for whom nothing is impossible.

When we are tired, afraid, or overwhelmed, our hearts can find rest, hope, and strength in God's name. "The name of the Lord is a fortified tower;

the righteous run to it and are safe" (Prov. 18:10). When we are filled with joy, celebrating and standing in the middle of unexpected blessings, we can rejoice in God's name. "Now, our God, we give you thanks, and praise your glorious name" (1 Chron. 29:13). Every moment of our lives, every circumstance we face, every emotion we feel—there is a name of God to meet our needs.

This is the miracle: God doesn't just give us what we want or even need; he gives us his very self. There is no ending to who he is and all the ways he loves us.

Name above All Names,

you are the One who is worthy of all our praise. Help us give everything we have and all we are to you, knowing you will never give us anything less in return. Amen.

Acknowledgments

Thank you to my family, especially my mom, dad, and grandmother Eula Armstrong, for teaching me from such a young age about who God is and how he loves us. I'm grateful for your prayers, support, and examples.

I'm also grateful for my publishing partners at Revell, especially Jen Leep, Wendy Wetzel, Amy Ballor, and Amylynn Warners. It's a joy to do work and ministry with you!

Mark Gerth, I'm so glad to be married to you. You love me at my worst and best, which helps me believe God does the same.

Lovelle Gerth-Myers, you are my daughter and a gracious gift from God who has taught me so much about his heart and how he writes our stories in mysterious, beautiful ways. I'm so thankful.

To all my friends who pray for, encourage, and have coffee with me—thank you for walking alongside me on this Word journey. You are the hands and ears of God to me so often.

I love all of you.

More Resources

Thank you so much for going on this journey to discover more of who God is and how he loves us!

If you'd like more encouragement, you can find it in Holley's other books, such as *You're Already Amazing*. If you'd like content to do with a group, check out the *You're Already Amazing LifeGrowth Guide*.

You can also stop by holleygerth.com for more content, tools, and resources. While you're there, you can sign up for devotional messages to be sent right to your inbox. And you can find Holley on Facebook, Instagram, Twitter, and Pinterest.

Holley is passionate about empowering girls in poverty to grow up to be fiercehearted women. You can find out more at compassion.com/fiercehearted.

Holley's cheering you on as you continue to grow closer to the God who loves you!

Notes

Chapter 1 Beginning and End

1. "How Many Babies Are Born Each Day?" The World Counts, June 13, 2014, accessed April 28, 2017, http://www.theworldcounts.com/stories/How-Many -Babies-Are-Born-Each-Day.

2. "How Many People Are Born/Die Every Day in the World? What Is Birth to Death Ratio in the World?," Quora.com, accessed April 28, 2017, https://www.quora .com/How-many-people-are-born-die-every-day-in-the -world-What-is-birth-to-death-ratio-in-the-world.

Chapter 2 Author

1. *Merriam-Webster*, s.v. "Author," accessed April 28, 2017, https://www.merriam-webster.com/dictionary /author.

Chapter 4 Bright Morning Star

1. Richard Talcott, "Venus Shines at Its Brightest be-fore Dawn," Astronomy.com, January 31, 2014, http://

www.astronomy.com/observing/sky-events/2014/01
/venus-shines-at-its-brightest-before-dawn.

Chapter 5 Counselor

1. Henry Cloud, *The Power of the Other: The Startling Effect Other People Have on You, from the Boardroom to the Bedroom and Beyond—and What to Do about It* (New York: HarperCollins, 2016), chap. 2, Kindle.

Chapter 6 Creator

1. Katrina Nannestad, *When Mischief Came to Town* (New York: Houghton Mifflin Harcourt, 2015), 162–63.

Chapter 8 Helper

1. Sharon Jaynes, *How Jesus Broke the Rules to Set You Free: God's Plan for Women to Walk in Power and Purpose* (Eugene, OR: Harvest House, 2015), 16.

Chapter 9 I Am

1. Elmer L. Towns, *The Ultimate Guide to the Names of God: Three Bestsellers in One Volume* (Grand Rapids: Baker Publishing Group, 2014), 224.

Chapter 10 Abba

1. Matthew George Easton, "Abba," in *Easton's Bible Dictionary* (Nashville: Thomas Nelson, 1997), http://www.biblestudytools.com/dictionaries/eastons-bible-dictionary/abba.html.

Chapter 12 Shepherd

1. Chuck Wooster, *Living with Sheep: Everything You Need to Know to Raise Your Own Flock* (Lanham, MD: Lyons Press, 2007), chap. 9, Kindle.

Chapter 19 Tear-Catcher

1. Sheila Walsh, "A Bottle of Your Tears," FaithGateway, August 4, 2015, http://www.faithgateway.com /bottle-of-your-tears/.

Chapter 29 Hiding Place

1. Christy Nockels, "2016 Wrap Up." Podcast, December 23, 2016, in *The Glorious in the Mundane*, podcast, https://christynockels.com/ep-21-2016-year-end/.
2. Nockels, "2016 Wrap Up."

Chapter 31 Cornerstone

1. Towns, *The Ultimate Guide to the Names of God*, 228.

Chapter 32 Carpenter

1. Ted Olsen, "The Life and Times of Jesus of Nazareth: Did You Know?," *Christian History*, accessed April 10, 2017, http://www.christianitytoday.com/history /issues/issue-59/life-times-of-jesus-of-nazareth-did-you -know.html.
2. Holley Gerth, "God-Sized Dreams . . . When You Worry You've Wasted Your Life," HolleyGerth.com, June 21, 2010, http://holleygerth.com/god-sized-dreams-when -you-worry-youve-wasted-your-life/.

Chapter 43 Faithful

1. Yagana Shah. "America's 'Longest-Married Couple' Wants to Give You Love Advice," Huffington Post, February 10, 2016, http://www.huffingtonpost.com/entry /longest-married-couple-will-answer-your-questions -about-love_us_56bb4e72e4b0b40245c4c0a3.

2. Shah, "America's 'Longest-Married Couple.'"

3. Mary Bowerman, "Here's What a Couple Married for 83 Years Can Teach You about Lasting Love," *USA Today*, February 23, 2016, https://www.usatoday.com /story/news/nation-now/2016/02/11/longest-married -couple-lasting-love-83-years/80174394/.

4. Suzannah Weiss, "Relationship Advice from America's Longest-Married Couple." *Glamour*, February 17, 2016, http://www.glamour.com/story/relationship -advice-from-the-w?mbid=social_fb_fanpage.

Chapter 46 Caretaker

1. "Cast All Your Care on the Lord!" Renner Ministries, May 11, 2016, http://www.renner.org/worry /cast-all-your-care-on-the-lord/.

Chapter 47 Rest

1. Marilyn Elias, "People's Views on Time Affect Health, Wealth, Relationships," *USA Today*, August 5, 2008, http://usatoday30.usatoday.com/news/health /2008-08-04-time-paradox-happiness_N.htm.

2. Walter A. Elwell, "Rest," in *Evangelical Dictionary of Theology* (Grand Rapids: Baker Books, 1996), http:// www.biblestudytools.com/dictionary/rest/.

Chapter 51 Word

1. Holley Gerth, "What Works Better than Worry," HolleyGerth.com, May 30, 2017, http://holleygerth.com /better-than-worry/.

About Holley

Holley Gerth can often be found at a quiet corner table in a coffee shop with an almond milk latte and her banged-up, beloved laptop. She's the *Wall Street Journal* bestselling author of *You're Already Amazing* and *Fiercehearted: Live Fully, Love Bravely*.

Holley is also a licensed counselor, certified life coach, and speaker who loves encouraging the hearts of women with words.

Holley is wife to Mark and, because God writes crazy-beautiful stories, mama to Lovelle and nana to Ellie. Until you can join Holley for your favorite coffee or tea, she'd love for you to hang out with her at http://holleygerth.com/.

CONNECT WITH
Holley

HOLLEYGERTH.COM

@HolleyGerth

"Holley Gerth turns words like a poet. Warm and personal, *You're Already Amazing* is a biblical, practical handbook for every woman's heart."

—Emily P. Freeman, author of *Grace for the Good Girl*

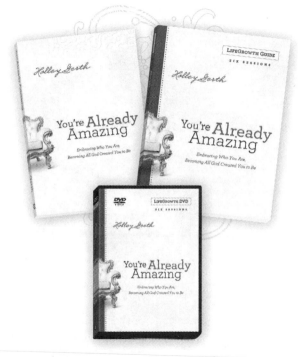

To learn more, visit HolleyGerth.com/Amazing.

All-new devotions to remind you of
what's true about you

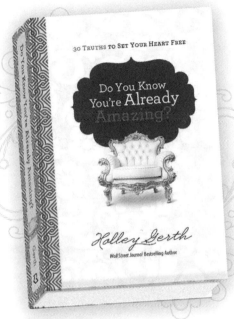

In this brand-new devotional, Holley Gerth invites you
to explore 30 truths God wants to whisper to your heart
about who you are created to be. Discover the freedom and
victory that come from knowing that you really are already
loved, valuable, and amazing.

Discover the dreams God has given you—
and then dare to pursue them.

Holley Gerth takes you by the heart and says, "Yes! You can do this!"
She guides you with insightful questions, action plans to take
the next steps, and most of all, the loving hand of a friend.

If your life isn't perfect . . .
If you've ever been disappointed . . .
If you feel stressed or tired . . .
This is for you.

"Holley Gerth is a fresh voice for every woman—
she echoes the voice of our Father."

—Ann Voskamp, *New York Times* bestselling
author of *One Thousand Gifts*